Vera Peiffer is a qualified analytical hypnotherapist and health kinesiologist with a highly successful private practice in London and Surrey. She also runs workshops for Positive Thinking and Stress Management in England, Germany and Italy and is principal of the The Peiffer Foundation, an organization which is concerned with teaching practical life skills.

If you would like more information on seminars or the Positive Thinking Correspondence Course, you can contact Vera at:

The Peiffer Foundation
39 Minniedale
Surbiton
Surrey KT5 8DH
Email: positive@blueyonder.co.uk
www.icet.net/peiffer-foundation.htm

By the same author

More Positive Thinking
Positively Single
Positively Fearless

positive
thinking

Everything you have always known
about positive thinking but were afraid
to put into practice

Vera Peiffer

Thorsons

Thorsons
An Imprint of HarperCollins*Publishers*
77–85 Fulham Palace Road,
Hammersmith, London W6 8JB

The Thorsons website address is:
www.thorsons.com

and *Thorsons*
are trademarks of
HarperCollins*Publishers* Limited

First published by Element 1989
This edition published by Thorsons 2001

3 5 7 9 10 8 6 4

A catalogue record for this book
is available from the British Library

ISBN 0 00 713099 6

Printed and bound in Great Britain by
Martins the Printers Ltd, Berwick-upon-Tweed

For Nada and Ljuba

Contents

Foreword – Please Do Not Read

▼ ▼ ▼ ▼

Excuse me, have you had this trouble with your eyesight long? No trouble with your eyesight. I see. In that case, would you please read the heading again? OK, now just skip the foreword and go on to the next chapter. Thank you.

I don't believe this. You're still reading on when I specifically asked you not to!

You see, when I started working on this book, a friend asked me how far I'd got with my writing and I replied that I had just started on the foreword. My friend waved a contemptuous hand and assured me that she certainly never read any forewords and, as far as she was aware, nobody else did either. That got me thinking. Since I wanted my foreword to be read I thought why not use it to prove a point?

The fact that you were *not* supposed to read the foreword made it practically irresistible – after all, you're still reading now, aren't you?

Note: The harder you try to avoid something, the less you can do it.

You will encounter the implications of these notes throughout the book, and I will demonstrate in the following chapters how they work and how you can use them to your advantage. What is more I know that you will succeed in making the findings of this book work for you, provided you *act* on your intention of getting more out of life and therefore put these findings into practice.

Theoretical knowledge is a marvellous thing. It increases your self-esteem, impresses your friends and looks good on your CV. All this is also very useful and certainly desirable, but theoretical knowledge cannot effect change: it will never change you from a miserable person into a happy one or from an unsuccessful person into a successful one.

In order to change your life for the better, you need more than just theoretical knowledge. You need to put these theories into practice. This, of course, means that you have to assume responsibility for your own well-being and stop blaming everyone else for things that go wrong in your life. This is not easy, because, let's face it, it is just so much more convenient to blame your parents/the Government/the weather for the fact that you cannot cope with certain aspects of life, rather than admit that you have not been pulling your weight and are therefore still stuck in that same old job, are still without a partner or still as miserable as you were two years ago.

In the long run, taking responsibility for your actions is a winning strategy because it opens the door to a completely new range of possibilities for becoming a successful person. When I am speaking of success I am speaking of a number of different areas, like health, wealth, happiness and personal fulfilment.

There are practically no limits to what you can achieve provided you put your mind to it. Reading this book will help, but you still have to go out and put the theories into practice. This ultimate step lies with you and you alone. Get on with it *now*; don't wait for the 'right moment', it may never come.

Note: The best time to act on new resolutions is now (not the 1st January).

I know you can do it!

VERA PEIFFER

Part

One

1 Mind over matter: The Pendulum Experiment

▼ ▼ ▼ ▼

Before we get into theoretical discussions of how the mind works, I would like you to try the following experiment.

Find a piece of string and tie a ring to one end of it. It is quite unimportant what sort of string you use or what kind of object you tie to the end – if you don't have a ring, use a key or a pen with a clip. The main thing is that you can fasten it somehow to the end of your string.

Now tie the other end of the string around your right index finger. As it is important to keep your right hand perfectly still, I suggest you sit down at a table, firmly rest both elbows on the table and support your right wrist with your left hand.

Lower your right index finger to allow the object to rest on the table, then gently lift the index finger again so that the object hangs still. *It is of the utmost importance that you do not move your hand while you carry out this experiment.*

Now fix your gaze on the object and begin to imagine that the pendulum starts swinging from left to right. See the movement in your mind, imagine how the object begins to swing, left to right, left to right. Say it silently to yourself, 'Left to right to left to right', and you will see that the pendulum actually begins to swing from left to right. It will begin to swing very slightly first, so keep on imagining, seeing in your mind's eye how the movement is becoming more pronounced, and you will see that this, too, will happen.

Now lower your hand once more, resting the object on the surface of the table. Again, lift the object away from the surface gently so that it hangs free, and now imagine that it begins to swing around in a clockwise circle. Move your eyes in a clockwise circle around the object, *see* the movement, and very slowly you will notice that the pendulum begins to swing accordingly. All the while make sure you do not move the hand that is holding the pendulum.

Of course you can also make the pendulum swing in an anti-clockwise circle or away from you and towards you. The result is always the same: the pendulum follows the imagined direction. Fascinating, isn't it?

However, before you give up your job to become a world-famous stage artist in the pendulum-swinging field, let us just have a look at what has been happening here. You were determined to hold your hand perfectly still, and, at the same time, imagined that the pendulum would begin to move in a particular direction. In other words, your will-power was in conflict with your imagination.

> **Note: When your will-power conflicts with your imagination, your imagination will always win out.**

Just consider another example. I am sure you know someone who has attempted their driving test and failed, although they were perfectly capable of doing their three-point turn and manoeuvring the car into a parking space under non-test conditions. The 'nerves' these people display in the test situation are nothing but the conflict between will-power and imagination. They *want* to pass the test, they *want* to perform well … but they *imagine* that they will fail and, as we have seen with the pendulum experiment, the imagination is more powerful than the will, and, consequently, the candidate tenses up, panics, and fails his or her driving test. In order to support your wishes effectively, you have to make sure that your imagination runs along the same lines as your wish, but more of this later.

So, what are you going to do if your pendulum didn't swing and you are now red in the face and contemplating using the pages of this book to wrap your sandwiches in?

> **Note: Never give up.**

The difference between a successful person and an unsuccessful person is that the successful person goes on where the unsuccessful person gives up. So, try again!

You may not be in the habit of using your imagination very often, but it is certainly a skill that can be acquired by practising. Children tend to have very good imaginations, so if you have lost the ability as an adult, you will simply have to re-learn it by using it more often. Using your imagination is a bit like riding a bicycle: you don't ever completely forget it. (You will find an exercise for improving your imagination on page 24.)

2 | The Subconscious Mind

▼ ▼ ▼ ▼

The mind, just like an iceberg, consists of two parts: like the tip of the iceberg, there is the *conscious mind*, which helps us with daily decision-making processes and also assists us with new situations where we have to apply rational thinking to fathom out what to do and how to do it. On the other hand, there is the *subconscious mind*, which makes up the far greater part, just like the submerged part of the iceberg. The subconscious mind deals with the repetitions of learned behaviour. This can be very helpful because it enables us to deal with situations more quickly when they occur again. Once we have learned to deal with a situation we find it easier next time around because we are using information that is already stored. For example, once we have learned that the oven door is hot we will use a cloth to open it the next time we have to do it, rather than burn our fingers again; once we know how to change gear in the car, we don't have to consciously think about it any more because the stored information comes up automatically as soon as the situation arises again; once we have learned where the letters are on a computer keyboard, we can type without looking because we have formed a mental picture in our subconscious mind of what the keyboard looks like.

Information from the conscious mind feeds directly into the subconscious mind. There is a strong link between the two parts of the mind. Everything you have ever seen, heard or experienced is perceived by the conscious mind and then stored away into the subconscious mind as a memory. This memory is stored as the incident itself *plus* the feeling that went with it at the time.

Let us assume you are bitten by a dog. You live through the actual incident and experience all the feelings of shock, hurt and anxiety that accompany the event. That incident and those feelings now get stored away in the subconscious. This memory influences your behaviour in similar situations.

Next time you see a dog you will act according to your memory pattern, that is, you will experience anxiety when you walk past a dog or, if the shock at the time was particularly strong, you may even cross over to the other side of the street to avoid the dog.

Let me give you another example. Let us assume that someone tells you repeatedly that you are useless. This other person can be your father, mother, husband, wife, girlfriend, boyfriend, boss or anybody who is in a position of authority or very close to you. The accusation can be unfounded or exaggerated, but if it is repeated over and over again, it will still get stored away in your subconscious mind, and, once again, the feeling of anger, resignation or depression you feel will go with it.

When the other person is given the opportunity to repeat their accusation over and over again over a long period of time, you will begin to feel that you really *are* useless and incapable of doing anything right because that is the automatic message you get from your subconscious whenever a new situation arises where you have to prove yourself.

You are now entering a vicious circle: because you believe you are useless, you will act out that belief; because you do not tackle any new situations you feel like a failure, and therefore you fail, and now the initial accusation has become true, like a self-fulfilling prophecy, *even though you may never have been useless in the first place.*

These two examples demonstrate that there is a link between the information or events we experience consciously (facts), the consequent subconscious storing of the event together with the accompanying feelings (memory) and the subsequent way we act (behaviour) when we find ourselves in the same situation again.

When we find that, for some reason, we cannot cope with a situation, this will leave our subconscious mind with a piece of negative information, with a memory trace of failure, and when the same or similar situation presents itself again, we will automatically assume that we are unable to cope. This assumption means that we are *expecting* things to go wrong again, we *imagine* ourselves incapable of handling the situation and, therefore, we will ultimately be unable to escape what we have imagined.

Note: Once the fact-memory-behaviour chain has been established, it works automatically.

There is, of course, also the possibility that you can no longer recall the incident itself, but you will nevertheless still experience the feeling that went with it as soon as you encounter a similar situation. You may well have forgotten that you were bitten by a dog at the age of two, but your subconscious mind will 'remind' you of the incident by emitting that feeling of fear that went with it at the time.

Feelings do not overcome us out of the blue, they are always linked to a real incident, which we may very well have forgotten, for whatever reason. The stronger the negative feeling that accompanied the event, the more likely it is that the incident has been repressed, that is, the more likely it is that we no longer remember it.

Note: Feelings that have been stored away in the memory will always be discharged as behaviour.

The good news is that the fact-memory-behaviour chain also works in a positive way. If you have been told that you are loved, even when you make mistakes, then your subconscious mind will register this information as a feeling of security, together with the message that you are loved no matter what, and you will then go and try out new things without being too frightened about the outcome because you know that, even if it does not work out, your sense of security and self-esteem will still be intact.

You will have noticed that I emphasise that information has to be given *repeatedly* before it takes root in the subconscious mind and that an incident has to be accompanied by a *particularly strong emotion* to impress itself on the subconscious and thus influence consequent behaviour.

These are points that are important to bear in mind:

Note: The more often a message is repeated, the deeper it is impressed on the subconscious.

Note: The stronger the emotion accompanying an event, the stronger that emotion is impressed on the subconscious.

3 | **What is Positive Thinking?**

▼ ▼ ▼ ▼

Positive Thinking is making use of the suggestibility of your subconscious mind in a positive way. We have seen in the previous chapters that information passes from the conscious mind to the subconscious.

The subconscious mind does not reason, it does not judge whether the information is right or wrong, sensible or silly, true or false, it just stores it like a faithful servant, only to produce behaviour at a later stage that accords with the stored information.

If we want to influence our behaviour or our performance, we have to do so via our subconscious mind, and that means we have to select new, positive thoughts that we consciously and repeatedly feed into our conscious mind because repeated thoughts take root in the subconscious mind. Repeated negative thoughts will influence it negatively and negative results will materialise as thoughts, wishes and ideas are translated into reality by the subconscious mind. We have to turn these round so that positive behaviour results.

Note: The quality of your thoughts determines the quality of your life.

You really and truly are what you think. Consider the following situation. It is 7.30 a.m. You have just woken up. As you begin to open your eyes, your conscious mind slowly moves into gear and you begin to think about the day that lies in front of you. You think about a meeting you will have to attend in the morning where you have to concede that you were unable to solve a particularly urgent problem, and, on top of this, you will have to confront a troublesome customer in the afternoon. It is still 7.30 in the morning. Nothing has actually happened yet, but you are already in a bad mood.

I can hear loud cries of protest now of, 'I would like to see you in my place, having to face that crowd of uncooperative half-wits!', or, 'If you're so clever why don't *you* come and try to deal with my customer! He does nothing but shout all the time!', and so on. But, just a minute. I'm not denying that the meeting is difficult and your customer an awkward person, but what I *am* saying is that you will not do yourself any favours by being in a bad mood on *top* of all that, because that only makes things more difficult.

If you are in a bad mood, you are simply not at your best. You are tense, irritable and, therefore, out of control. You cannot concentrate, you are frightened and you feel panicky. And, of course, the story does not end there. Because you are in a bad mood, you may be particularly monosyllabic or grumpy at breakfast, which is not going to endear you to the family. You will be a touch unfriendly with your colleagues at work who, in turn, will possibly comment on your mood and that will *really* get your back up ('Why don't they mind their own business?') – and then the meeting is postponed until next week. This is possibly the worst thing that could happen, because it means that you will have another week's worrying to do until it is finally over. Or, if the meeting *does* take place that day, you have already spent all your valuable energy on getting worked up. In the evening you will go home, exhausted, kick the dog and wonder whether you are really being paid enough for this demanding job …

By this time, something should dawn on you. Yes, I'm going to say it: *you* are responsible for wasting your energy in this manner – *it is not the job, it is you!* It was your negative thinking first thing in the morning that got you started on the wrong track.

There is nothing you can do about certain events in your life – meetings will occur, customers will sometimes be difficult – but you can certainly do something about the way you choose to *look* at these events. By putting yourself into a positive frame of mind, you will not only feel better within yourself, but you will also cope better with the event, and, above all, you will influence your environment positively. People like being with a relaxed, happy person and your positive attitude will soon be reflected in the way other people treat you.

Note: Whatever you send out to others will come back to you like a boomerang.

The above note is true – always. It is just a matter of time before you reap what you have sowed. This is true for all areas, be it in private life or business.

Being positive means being open and friendly. It does not mean being anybody's doormat. It means saying what you want and going for it. It does not mean being a bully. Being positive means consciously choosing to look on the bright side. It does not mean seeing the world through unrealistic rose-tinted spectacles. Being positive means liking yourself and others, it means taking an interest in the people around you.

Note: A person who is interested is interesting.

Being positive means worrying less and enjoying more, choosing to look at the good side rather than filling your mind with gloom and doom, choosing to be happy rather than unhappy. It is your foremost duty to make sure that you feel good within yourself.

Note: It is of fundamental importance that you look after yourself and work on achieving happiness for yourself.

If you think the above note is selfish, then look at it from another angle. Unless you are happy yourself, you can't make anyone else happy, nor can you be of help to others, nor will you be successful in what you're doing. Imagine a miserable psychoanalyst trying to dissuade a client from suicide. Imagine a bad-tempered salesman trying to sell his product to a customer. Imagine a grumpy husband trying to keep his marriage going.

So how happy are you? Let's take stock.

Ten-Minute Solitaire

Try the following. Sit down in a room all by yourself, with no radio or television on, and don't do anything for ten minutes.

Ten minutes can be an eternity to sit doing nothing, without any distractions, when you don't like yourself. It forces you to confront potentially unpleasant thoughts about yourself and, ultimately, prevents you from relaxing and switching off.

Many people, particularly women, feel guilty about relaxing or wanting to be on their own. They tend to interpret the word 'relaxing' as 'sitting around not doing anything productive', and 'wanting to be by myself' as 'being unsociable and therefore uncaring'. Do you recognise these thoughts, ladies? If you do, it is time you changed your attitude.

In the following pages, you will find exercises for physical and mental relaxation (pages 24–6), as well as the analyses of a number of particular problems (pages 47–9).

It may well be that you have to start dealing with your particular problem before you are able to relax. Try the relaxation exercises first, though, because they will give you an indication of your present frame of mind, and then repeat them after you have worked through your problem. As you are getting to grips with the problem, you will find that your ability to relax increases.

Part
Two

4 | What Is On Your Mind?

▼ ▼ ▼ ▼

I would like you to start off by paying attention to what you are thinking throughout the day. Check the quality of your thoughts. Do you find yourself indulging in destructive thoughts, such as hatred, guilt, anger or envy? Nip them in the bud and replace them with positive thoughts.

If you do not get rid of negative thoughts straight away, they begin to grow and get out of proportion. Listen to yourself thinking. You will be surprised by your tendency to think negatively whenever a particular situation arises. Make a point of never thinking a negative thought to the end. As soon as you find yourself going off on the negative thoughts track, say 'STOP' in your mind and replace them with positive thoughts.

Here are some classic negative thoughts and some ways of re-thinking them positively.

- **Making a strength out of a weakness**

  Negative
  'God, I wish I didn't have to go to this party tonight. I never know what to say to new people.'

  Positive
  'I am looking forward to going to this party tonight and meeting some interesting people. I like other people and I'm a good listener. Other people enjoy talking to me.'

- **Stop being a victim**

  Negative
  'I'm annoyed/anxious because my boss has still not told me whether I'm going to get that salary increase.'

Positive
'I deserve my salary increase. I have allowed enough time for my boss to make up his mind, therefore I can confidently go and ask him about his decision today.'

Negative
'I feel cheated. My cleaning lady never does the windows.'

Positive
'My cleaning lady is doing a good job except for the windows. I can point out this fact to her in a friendly but clear manner.' (If your cleaning lady comes into the house while you are away at work, leave a note or ring her up. Unless you speak about it, nothing will change.)

- ## Looking after yourself

Negative
'Life has passed me by. Nothing good ever happens to me.'

Positive
'Today is the first day of the rest of my life. Today things are different. I have decided to treat myself to a little luxury (walk in the country/cinema/sauna/ nice meal), I deserve it!'

Negative
'I'm totally shattered, but I can't relax because I still have to do the dishes.'

Positive
'I am in control. I decide when I want to do the washing up. I'm tired now, so my priority is to rest. I deserve it. The washing up can wait until later/ tomorrow/next week.'

- ## Self-image

Negative
'I'm afraid of the presentation I have to give next week. Everyone will be watching and I'll be totally flustered.'

Positive
'I'm well prepared for my presentation. I know what I want to say and I look forward to sharing my knowledge with others. Other people are interested in what I have to say.'

(It is obviously important to do your homework. No amount of positive thinking will help you succeed if you have not prepared for your presentation.)

There are a few rules you should observe when you make up your new, positive thoughts.

• **Avoid negative phrasing**

Don't say 'I won't be frightened', say 'I am calm and relaxed'; in other words, think about what you *want*, not about what you *don't* want.

• **Use the present tense**

Try and avoid future tense if possible. Say 'I am confident when I speak in front of other people', rather than, 'I will be confident when I speak to others'. Your subconscious mind takes things literally, so if you are talking of something occurring in the future, your subconscious will wait with you for the future, but it is important that you feel confident *now* in order to feel confident when the event actually takes place.

• **Use your new positive thoughts repeatedly**

You will see that the old negative thoughts keep cropping up when you are 'not watching'. Old habits die hard, and you will have to persist in replacing them every single time you catch yourself. You will see, though, that eventually your efforts are rewarded: positive thoughts begin to appear automatically, and constructive thinking becomes second nature.

• **Start today**

In a previous example I stated that your thoughts first thing in the morning determine how your day will turn out for you. Here are a few examples of how you can programme yourself for a successful day.

  • 'I look forward to a good day. I am competent and open to new ideas, and I deal with all my tasks efficiently and easily.'

- 'I like myself and others. I work well with others, I am constructive and willing to co-operate, and I find it easy to win the co-operation of others.'
- 'I am an easy-going person. I approach problems in a calm and relaxed manner. I see problems as springboards into new ideas. They help me develop new skills.'
- 'Today is a day of harmony. I am in harmony with the world around me. I can see my aims clearly and I know that I can reach them easily.'
- 'Today is a wonderful day that brings me lovely surprises. I'm a lucky person. I attract good luck like a big magnet.'

These are just a few examples. Choose the one that you feel happiest with, combine several, alter them so that they fit your personal situation. Just make sure you follow the rules on page 17.

You may find it helpful to write your positive thoughts down on a piece of paper and read them several times during the day. After reading them a few times you will know them by heart. Keep on repeating them to yourself over and over again so that they become firmly imprinted in the subconscious mind.

A word of warning: when you start repeating any of these positive mottos to yourself you may feel rather silly. While you are saying to yourself, 'Today is a wonderful day' this little voice will whisper to you 'No it isn't! It's raining and I don't feel like going to work.' These interrupting negative thoughts can come up quite frequently in the beginning. It is as if an old tape is playing in your mind, and the old tape appears to ridicule your new thoughts ('Who do you think you're kidding? I know it's *not* a wonderful day!'). At this early stage there is a great temptation to give up. Nobody likes to feel ridiculous, not even when they are on their own, but as a positive thinker, you are of course no longer in the league of giver-uppers.

To help you get over this initial difficulty, just use this trick. Pretend that you are playing a part. Pretend you are another person, a new person who is determined and confident, calm and collected. Choose a model and pretend that you *are* that person. Surely Superman never worries whether his glamorous outfit will materialise or whether he will be left in his underpants when he takes his whirl in the phone booth? Well, just make out you are Superman or

Superwoman for that matter. *Act* confidently, even though your feelings may contradict you. *Insist* on being right about changing your thought patterns for the better. This first step is just for yourself: before you can convince other people of your new positive image, you have to convince yourself. Here's how to go about it.

- Stand in front of the mirror and give yourself a winning smile.
- Tell yourself that, from today on, things are changing for the better.
- Tell yourself that you are making a fresh start. Whatever anybody said about you in the past is null and void. From now on *you* decide what you think about yourself and you choose to think *well* of yourself.
- Keep repeating your new motto, even if someone beats you to the last seat on the tube. You are *not* kidding yourself by doing so. You are simply making sure that you preserve your energy. You are about to achieve great things, and you will not allow yourself to be held back by trivialities.

5 | Getting in Touch With Your Subconscious Mind

▼ ▼ ▼ ▼

Your subconscious mind is not only concerned with storing memories and feelings, it is also the seat of creativity, intuition and ideas, all of which are intangibles.

Intuition appears suddenly, pointing you in a particular direction. An idea springs up in your mind while you are mowing the lawn and, within a second, you have the solution to a problem you have been thinking about for days. Your subconscious mind has helped you create a solution.

If you are an artist, your subconscious mind helps you in the same way: it provides you with an inspiration or creative idea for your next piece of work. Creative professions bring people more in touch with the subconscious than a lot of office jobs do. Creativity is mostly an undesirable item within the office environment as it tends to upset routine and sometimes is deemed to threaten the boss's authority, particularly if it was someone in the lower ranks who had the good idea and not the boss!

Good ideas are not always acknowledged or put into practice, and quite a few of you will be able to confirm that for every good idea there are at least ten people who tell you that it can't be done. Very often, routine is taking the place of flexibility, making your job and life in general much harder by setting unnecessary limits and making things boring.

Nowadays there exists a gross *over*-estimation of the achievements of the rational mind (which, as you will remember, only constitutes the minor part of our overall mental capacity) and an equally gross *under*-estimation of subconscious forces. We generally believe only what we can see and touch. We believe only things that are measurable and that are accompanied by tables filled with figures and experimental data. Creativity, intuition and ideas tend to rank fairly low (except for occasions where they have proved to make a lot of money) because they are not measurable and therefore officially do not exist. And yet, when we think about it, we see that everything that has ever been achieved started with an idea. Someone had a flash of intuition once and founded the company you are working for now. Someone had an idea once and started building the first car … and so on.

Note: Every achievement has started as an idea.

Think about it. What was it that made you buy this book? Maybe you saw the title or the cover and it gave you an idea of how to solve one of your problems? You probably went through the index to see whether there was a section on that problem, then began reading half a page into it and then bought the book.

Ideas can be sparked off by chance. They cannot be forced. Ideas have nothing to do with will-power. The harder you try to come up with an idea, the less you can do it. The more will-power you employ, the less likely is it that you will get to your subconscious. Ideas spring up as you are not looking, as you are thinking of something entirely different.

Equally, intuition has nothing to do with will-power. Intuition is a directive force within you that guides you in a seemingly irrational manner, and yet so often turns out to be right.

The subconscious mind is always working for you. Even when *you* have stopped thinking about a problem, your subconscious mind is still dealing with it, and when you are relaxed enough to listen to that inner voice, the subconscious will yield its solution in the shape of an intuition or an idea. This can occur either during the day or at night in a dream (albeit in a disguised form).

Dreams are a vehicle for discharging the anxieties and fears that you have accumulated during the day, thus enabling you to sleep. If it was not for your dreams, the anxieties would keep you awake and you would be unable to restore your energy by sleeping.

In order to make use of these subconscious facilities it is necessary to develop a sense for your 'inner voice'. It is most important to keep your rational mind in check, otherwise it takes over and blocks the subconscious mind. Constant worrying and the general indulging in 'disaster thoughts' make you singularly unreceptive to any constructive ideas.

If you want to take advantage of intuition and creative ideas, you need to learn to partially switch off the conscious mind. Without knowing it, you sometimes do this quite naturally. Remember the times when you sit at your desk and gaze out of the window, not really looking at anything in particular, not taking in what is going on in your environment, and just thinking of something quite intently so that you can practically see it in front of you. At these times, you have switched into a day-dreaming mode where your reasoning mind is somewhat drowsy and permits you to wander off into whatever feelings or thoughts present themselves at the time. While you are day-dreaming, you are totally absorbed and you sit perfectly still. You can only do that when you don't worry. As soon as you begin to worry you start fidgeting. Worrying is interference from your rational mind, and you need to keep it under control in order to benefit from your subconscious.

I would like you to try the following exercises so that you can:

- assess for yourself how easy or difficult you find it to relax
- become aware of the difference between being alert and being relaxed
- gain access to your subconscious mind.

Breathing Exercise

- Find yourself a comfortable position, either sitting or lying down.
- Uncross your legs and arms (crossing your legs and arms creates physical tension).

> *Note: Physical tension creates mental tension.*
> *Mental tension creates physical tension.*

- Put one hand on your stomach area, just above the navel.
- Check the main tension points and consciously relax them:
  - unclench your teeth
  - drop your shoulders
  - open your hands.
- Close your eyes and just be aware of the position of your body in the chair or on the bed. Concentrate on your head for a moment, then on your arms, the trunk of your body, your legs.

- Listen to your breathing for about ten breaths. Do not do anything. It is unimportant whether you breathe quickly or slowly, just listen to it.
- Now begin to take deeper breaths. As you breathe in, make sure you breathe in through your belly. If you are doing this properly, the hand on your stomach will rise with your expanding belly. As you exhale, your belly area will deflate and your hand sink down with it.
- Take ten deep breaths through your belly and for each one hold your breath for a count of five, then exhale again.
- Let your breathing go back to normal again.
- Gently tighten all your muscles and, as you release the tension, open your eyes again. You should feel physically calm now.

If you have problems

Are you finding it difficult to make your belly come out as you breathe in?
With your eyes open, try to make your belly round by pushing it out using your muscles. Leave your hand on your stomach so you know what it feels like. Now, combine pushing your muscles out with inhaling. Finally, try inhaling on its own again, making breathing the power that pushes out your belly.

Are you finding that you are not feeling relaxed at the end of the exercise?
Are you very worried about something? Any problems you have may well interfere with your exercise, making it more difficult to concentrate. This is normal. Do not resist these interfering thoughts, because resistance creates tension. Just say to yourself, 'I can feel that I'm worried about something – this is OK. I will go back to worrying immediately after finishing this exercise. I resume my exercise now.' Say this to yourself every time you find worrying thoughts interrupting your exercise.

Are you trying too hard to relax? Don't try to be perfect. This exercise will definitely *not* solve all your problems; it merely helps to take the edge off any physical tension you may be under, so don't expect to be comatose by the end of it! Doing this exercise is like taking a step back from everyday life, not more, not less.

Note: The harder you try to relax the less you can do it.

Are you angry at yourself for not relaxing better? Do you find it unbearable not to be the supreme champion at everything you are doing? Are you pushing yourself very hard at everything you attempt? If you have to answer yes to these questions, then it is high time you treated yourself better.

At the moment, you are over-critical and impatient, in other words, you are nasty to yourself. Don't be! You *deserve* a break and you have the right to make mistakes and have faults, just like everyone else. Treat yourself like a little baby: with much love and gentleness. Now try the exercise again. You will see that you are doing better this time.

You can do this exercise anywhere, on the bus, on the tube, while you are waiting at the dentist's, when you are exhausted and don't have time for a nap, when you are stressed. Breathing properly will help take the edge off anxiety, recharge your batteries and enable you to think clearly.

Breathing deeply means that the entire lungs (rather than just the top halves) are filled with air and that, as a result, more oxygen gets into the blood. Oxygen is needed by the brain to function properly. Furthermore, deep breathing loosens and relaxes the belly muscles and the solar plexus, which is the area around your stomach where a great number of nerves come together. Relaxation of the solar plexus means that your inner organs can work properly. By breathing deeply, you are creating physical harmony.

Mental Holiday Exercise

- Try this exercise immediately after the Breathing Exercise, or choose a time when you are reasonably relaxed anyway. You will have to practise Mental Holiday under non-stressful conditions before you are able to apply it in difficult situations, so perfectionists beware!
- Find yourself a comfortable position and close your eyes.
- Start off by remembering a suitcase or travelling bag of yours. In your mind, see it sitting on your bed, ready packed. As you are looking at the open suitcase, repeat the word 'holiday' to yourself. Get into the mood, hype yourself up. See the scene in your mind and feel the elation of going off to your favourite holiday spot. Money is no object, in fact, the more expensive the better.

- You are ready to go. Close your suitcase. Now you are at the airport, station or seaport (needless to say you got there by chauffeur-driven limousine), boarding your plane, train or ship.
- You have arrived at your holiday destination. It is superb and exactly as you would like it to be. In your mind, look at everything in detail – the mountains, sea, beach, trees, countryside, whatever you have chosen.

  See yourself moving around, enjoying the beauty of the scenery, *feel* that sense of elation at being in these gorgeous surroundings. Be there, get involved in your day-dream – make it a thoroughly pleasurable experience to be on this Mental Holiday.
- When you want to get back, just gently tense all your muscles, relax them again and open your eyes – and leave that smile on your face, it suits you!

If you have problems

Are you finding it difficult to imagine your ideal holiday?

Maybe you have not been using your imagination for a while and therefore you have become 'rusty'. In order to regain the ability to imagine or fantasise, start off with an object in your environment – a plant, the telephone, a picture, anything at all. Look at the object closely, observing every little detail.

Once you have done that, close your eyes and describe the item to yourself, recalling as many details as possible. Now open your eyes again and check whether you remembered the item accurately. The more often you practise this, the better you will become at picturing something in your mind. The fact that you can remember means that you have formed a mental picture of the item. You cannot describe anything that you cannot imagine. Improving your imagination will automatically improve your memory.

Are you finding it difficult to enjoy your holiday?

What marred your day-dream? Did you find it impossible to imagine something as entirely pleasurable, without any flaws? Perhaps you consider this exercise unrealistic and want to tell me that last time you went to Majorca you got landed in that grotty little place next to the main road where you suspect the maid must have taken your earrings because you couldn't find them anywhere … I'm afraid you didn't get the point of the exercise.

We all know that life is not perfect. There will always be ups and downs and unforeseen obstacles. This is so, whether we are happy or miserable about it. We cannot do anything about unpredictable events appearing in our lives, but we can certainly influence how we cope with them.

We have a choice of how we want to look at problems – positively or negatively. We have a choice whether to be happy or miserable. No matter what we choose, the problems will still occur, so we can either sit anxiously in a corner, waiting for the next thing to go wrong and be thoroughly unhappy with life or we can face problems as and when they appear, deal with them as best we can and have a thoroughly good time in the meanwhile. Besides, are you *quite* sure you didn't leave those earrings on the beach …?

Mental holiday is certainly an exercise in escapism, but then it is meant to be. Just like deep breathing, it gives body and mind a chance to relax and recover lost energy, and it helps you gain a bit of distance from everyday routine, leaving you refreshed and in a good mood. Mental holiday is meant to make you feel good, and only when you imagine something beautiful will you get the maximum result from this exercise.

6 Setting Up Your Personal Success Programme

▼ ▼ ▼ ▼

In this life, everyone gets what they deserve, but only the successful will admit it. There is no such thing as a heavenly department for the distribution of success. Each and every one of us has to work on achieving their own happiness and their own success.

Some people attending my workshops have been saying that they feel they are ruled by their environment, by their present financial situation, by their partner, their boss or by the type of job they are in, and they feel quite hopeless about their chances of success to change their life for the better. All the external factors seem to be so overpowering that their own endeavours appear to be doomed from the start.

When I ask these people what they have actually done to achieve their goal, it either transpires that they have not done anything at all because they thought it was not going to work anyway, or they lost courage after the first (and often feeble) attempt and gave up, despite the fact that they did not even encounter the resistance from the outside world that they had expected.

Change can be a frightening thing and, although your present situation may be unpleasant, it can still seem preferable to the hassles and upsets of setting foot into new territory and risking getting hurt as you are trying to deal with unfamiliar situations. It is a bit like the tooth that stops hurting as you sit in the dentist's waiting room. Suddenly you feel it is not that bad and really you should not be wasting your dentist's time; it probably is nothing. Or, if you have to discuss something difficult with a colleague, isn't it amazing how you start doing all your filing and the odd jobs in the office that you normally loathe, just to avoid having to speak to that colleague?

It is the same thing with making changes in our lives. We are afraid and try to avoid them, even though the results would be very positive for us. We like the sound of the end of the journey, but not the journey itself – God let me lose weight but don't make it hard to do.

Changing your life for the better means learning new things. This may not always be easy but it is certainly very gratifying and you will emerge at the end as a more confident and self-assured person. You will also find that, after a while, it becomes easier to tackle unsatisfactory situations, simply because you spend less time *worrying* and more time *acting*. You start to get up and do something about problems rather than procrastinate. Putting things off does not solve the problem, it just adds the problem of time.

There is little point in postponing working on being happy. When you were at school you told yourself, 'I will be happy once I have left school.' Then you left school and you thought, 'I will be happy once I get a job.' When you have a job you make your happiness conditional on having a wife or husband, a house, then on the children leaving home. Before you know it you are old and have to realise that life has passed you by. Many people waste their lives waiting for 'the' great happiness and overlook the many smaller happy events that occur on the way.

Don't allow this to happen to you. Start to enjoy your life *now*. When you begin to live in the here and now, rather than in the past or the future, you will discover a great many things that give you pleasure. All you have to do is begin to look for them and you will find them everywhere. Expect to be lucky today, and you will be lucky. Try it, it works.

On your way to a better life, your biggest enemy (next to yourself) is probably habit. We get so used to doing things in a certain way, to thinking along certain lines, to reacting so automatically to certain situations that it almost seems as if our mind switches into 'auto-pilot' in certain situations, and that is why it appears nearly impossible to change. As long as the habit is something fairly straightforward, like giving up smoking or cutting down on junk food, we can just about imagine that this is feasible, especially when we have just had lots of champagne and it is the 31st December and there is more champagne to come.

Breaking habits like worrying or bottling up anger, on the other hand, seem to be beyond our control because we believe that they are caused by external events. We feel we simply cannot give up worrying when our husbands or wives are not home on time. We feel we cannot possibly complain about a lousy meal in an expensive restaurant. Instead, we say, 'We'll just not come here again,' and then go home and stew over it for a whole week.

Excuses for not wanting to change abound, 'I *have* to worry because I *care* so much!', or, 'I mustn't complain because that would be *rude*'. Nonsense! Think about it. There is nothing you can achieve through worrying. If your husband has had an accident, you cannot change it. If your wife is having an affair, you would do better to ask her about it than to worry. If you complain in a restaurant, you do not have to be impolite. There is nothing wrong with pointing out that you were not impressed with a badly prepared meal. These habits *can* be changed. Others have done it, so why not you?

If you want to put your life into a more positive framework, here are some points that will need attention:

- Take responsibility for yourself, your actions and your feelings. They are yours, and you are the only person who can influence them. Don't wait for the outside world to change, because it won't.
- Take stock. What is your present situation? Go through every aspect – health, finances, job, partnership, self-image and so on. What points would you like to improve?
- Make a list of things you want to change and put them in order of priority. Tackle the points one by one – getting to grips with one point is better than making half-hearted attempts at several.
- Look at the first point on your list. What exactly is the problem? Take it apart and determine which are the external factors that come into play and which are your own attitudes that aggravate the situation. Let us assume you are fuming because three shop assistants are chatting while you are waiting to be served. The external factors are that the shop assistants don't do their job. The internal factor is that you are too timid to attract their attention. There will always be shop assistants who prefer chatting to working, but you do not have to be timid for the rest of your life.

    You will see that often there is not much you can do about the external factors. The point of attack must therefore lie in your own attitudes.

- Set yourself a target. Be precise about what you want. Don't say, 'I would like to be more popular', say 'I would like to feel more at ease when I go to parties'. Be realistic about your targets. Don't say, 'I want a figure like Kate Moss', say 'I want to lose that excess weight'.
- Start doing your groundwork. If your target is to finally tackle your driving test, you will have to practise your three-point turn. All the positive thinking in the world will not help you pass if you cannot do it before you go in for the test.

   If you want to attract a partner, make sure you look attractive. Curlers in your hair and a cigarette hanging from the corner of your mouth are not likely to drive a man wild with desire, any more than a stained shirt over a potbelly and the general appearance of a one-man slum will have women throwing themselves at your feet.
- Eliminate the expression 'I can't' from your vocabulary. If you say 'I can't' you are setting yourself limits. Think of the bumblebee. According to the laws of aerodynamics it is impossible to fly with the proportions of body-weight to wing area that it has, but the bumblebee doesn't know that and simply flies.

Note: You can because you think you can.

- Get ready physically and mentally. Make sure you are in the best frame of mind to start on your first point. Do one of the relaxation exercises on pages 24–8 everyday for at least three weeks. Get into the habit of relaxing at least once a day and you will see that it becomes easier to switch off. This will help you preserve your energy, which you will need for the tasks ahead.
- Begin your day by standing in front of the mirror and say to yourself, 'From now on, things are going to change for the better' and *mean* it.
- See yourself having achieved your aim. What you can imagine, you can do in reality. If you want to lose weight, see yourself in your mind as a slim person, see yourself wearing a new, smaller size outfit, imagine yourself in front of a mirror in this outfit and see the proud smile on your face.

   If you have been slimmer at one time, find a photograph and carry it around with you. Take out a skirt or a pair of trousers that are too tight now and leave them out for you to look at, saying to yourself, 'I am going to wear these again!'

Fill your mind with images of the new you. If you are a man who gets flustered when he is talking to women, imagine yourself engaged in a conversation, see yourself confident, speaking fluently, see your partner listening to you attentively, enjoying your conversation, see her smiling at you. See yourself as successful and you will *be* successful.

- Stop making excuses and start *now*.

7 Some Personality Traits and Their Strategies

▼ ▼ ▼ ▼

In this chapter you will see a variety of personality types and their respective idiosyncrasies.

Please note that there is hardly anybody who is entirely in one category – we are all made up of a variety of personality elements that have evolved over the years. Personality is something that we are born with but it is also subject to external influences.

If you have children, you will be able to confirm that personality is evident at a very early age. One baby will sleep through the night while another will cry frequently. One child is lively and curious and eager to learn, the other placid and quiet, developing rather late.

In the following years, a lot depends on the environment of that lively or placid child. If the liveliness is seen as a positive quality, then it is likely that the child will eventually learn to channel this energy in a useful way. If the liveliness is seen as desirable (which it usually is for boys, but not for girls) and the child is given total freedom to display this lively behaviour at all times, the child can become very unruly because it lacks boundaries.

If, on the other hand, parents and/or teachers define the lively child as hyperactive and naughty, the child may get into all sorts of trouble for its 'negative behaviour'. Punishment of some sort may follow a display of liveliness, and the child will learn to either suppress the behaviour or to start displaying the behaviour in an exaggerated way, thus provoking more punishment, which, in turn, makes the child behave in an even more disruptive way, until it has finally become the obnoxious little brat the parents have always told the child it was.

This is self-fulfilling prophecy *par excellence*.

Shyness, too, can be labelled in different ways. It can either be regarded as 'good manners', and therefore appropriate and desirable, or it can be scolded and punished as 'backward' and 'stupid'. How the child is subsequently treated and develops then depends on that initial labelling.

The child labelled as having 'good manners' may develop into a very inhibited person who is incapable of venting his or her feelings, be they good or bad. The child that is called 'backward' may develop an inferiority complex and never achieve anything. It is quite a job to get it right, isn't it? You might as well forgive your parents because you are bound to make mistakes yourself once you are a parent.

As influences coming from parents, siblings, teachers and classmates are particularly strong during childhood and adolescence, it stands to reason that the attitudes of the social environment will have a substantial impact on a young person's life. Since a six-year-old cannot just pack his bags and say, 'Right, I've had enough of being treated like an idiot! After all, I'm the only one round here who understands computers!' and walk out, he will have to keep on listening to parental complaints about his inadequacies until he *can* move out, which may not be for another ten years or more. By that time, the idea is firmly settled in his mind that he is no good.

Again, this is painting an extreme picture as most of us had a reasonable mixture of praise and disapproval during childhood. Yet, we do not seem to emerge from our cocoons of childhood without a bit of a struggle. Some events or remarks may have affected us more severely than we realised at the time, and they still exert their influence on us today. We all have our histories. We all have our struggles and so did our parents, who had to cope with their parents one way or another.

This does not mean that we are determined by our past forevermore, though. If you did not like the way your parents treated you, you can always choose friends who treat you differently once you are grown up. If you have reacted with great anger every time someone has accidentally jostled you in the street for the last 20 years, then it is going to take time and effort to get rid of this angry feeling, but you can do it, and it is a small price to pay for avoiding an ulcer.

In this chapter, you will find some personality traits described in an extreme way, nearly to the extent of caricature. You will rarely encounter people like that in reality, but what you may find are people that display a tendency towards one of the types to a greater or lesser extent.

These sketches are meant to help you look at yourself and determine where your weak points lie, which might require a dose of Positive Thinking. So, take the sketches with a pinch of salt and use them as a guideline. There is no need to throw yourself under a train because you collected most of your points in the backstabbing section. If you do then it just shows that you are honest with yourself, and that, in turn, is going to help you become the better person that you really are.

The Patroniser

The male or female Patroniser has a clear-cut picture of the world in his or her head. Whatever they hear, see or experience, they manage to label unambiguously as either good or bad, right or wrong. Patronisers have made up their mind once and for all which items belong in which category, and that is that. The Patroniser does not worry about any grey zones between the black and white areas in life.

Endowed with a loud voice, the Patroniser then proceeds to spread the gospel. Whether you want to hear it or not, the Patroniser will let you know what his or her opinion is on any given subject. If you have ever been to hospital you will recall that bossy nurse who stomps into your room at 5 a.m. to take your temperature, booming, 'Aren't we lazy? Still asleep! Come now, Mr Winterbottom, open your mouth!' And if you want to know what these new tablets are that she has just given you, she will look at you reproachfully and reply, 'Now we *must* follow doctor's orders, mustn't we, Mr Winterbottom?' In other words, she is putting you in your place because, according to her book, the patient is not allowed to question the doctor's (or her) authority, and that's what you have just been doing.

Note also the permanent use of 'we' instead of 'you'. You are no longer a person in your own right and, anyway, nurse knows best, so she takes you under her matronly but infuriatingly patronising wing, integrating your person into her own. Thus, 'we' is born.

Criticism comes hard and fast with Patronisers, and it is not always constructive. Even though they have good ideas, people tend to reject their suggestions purely because of the way they are put across.

The Patroniser's Good Points
The Patroniser is often truly knowledgeable and genuinely interested in helping others.

The Patroniser's Problem Points
The Patroniser tends to be rigid in his outlook. Often, the opinions held have been developed early in life and have not been checked against reality since. Patronisers can be a bit old-fashioned and are part of that group of people who still think that the microchip is a by-product of the recession for potato farmers.

Patronisers are so sure of their opinions that they tend to deliver sermons rather than enter into a dialogue with others. Patronisers are also not aware that they are hurting other people's feelings ('It's only for your own good!') when they are so harshly criticising them, and that makes them unpopular because people either dislike or fear them.

The Patroniser's Inner State
Rigid opinions are a sign of fundamental insecurity. If the world seems a frightening and confusing place, then a rigid thought structure can provide a sort of safety rail to cling to. This rigidity, though, has its drawbacks. Bridges and even skyscrapers are built so that they can sway slightly in a very strong wind, and it is precisely this flexibility that prevents them from collapsing in a storm. The same is true for people. It is the ones that are able to adapt to new situations that fare best.

Patronisers tend to waste a lot of energy resisting change and sometimes miss out on opportunities that could be to their advantage, simply because they do not fit into their concepts and therefore frighten them ('I'm not having any of these new-fangled computers in *my* office, thank you very much!').

The Mouse

The Mouse is a walking apology. Even nowadays they are mostly women, and Mice feel that they have to apologise for having been born and if they had their own way, their gravestones would say 'Excuse my dust'.

Mice are afraid that they are in the way or that they are causing inconvenience to others. They will wait for half an hour for two shop assistants to finish their chat rather than draw attention to themselves.

The Mouse hovers a lot, in every respect. She hovers to wait on her family, she hovers for her boss to call her in for dictation, she hovers when she is asked for her opinion because she feels unable to come down on one or the other side of the fence. Even if a Mouse tried to sit on the fence, she would probably fall off it, so sure is she that she is useless (and as we know by now, if you *think* you are useless you will eventually *become* useless).

Mice are not necessarily popular because their readiness to oblige is often considered stupidity, and their constant apologies make people fed up with them rather than like them. The word 'no' might just as well not exist for Mice because they would not dream of uttering it, ever.

The Mouse's Good Points
The Mouse is helpful, considerate and a great comfort to people in need. The Mouse usually has a lot of compassion for others (which, however, is not the same thing as insight), and shows untiring support for those who are ill or disadvantaged in any way. Little old ladies refer to the Mouse as an 'angel'.

With people needing help the Mouse feels safe and develops skills that come as a pleasant surprise to herself and others. As these points are advantageous to others, they are usually promoted as desirable.

It has to be emphasised, though, that if helpful behaviour is carried out in a self-effacing way, without considering one's own health or well-being, then it ceases to be positive and starts to become self-destructive.

The Mouse's Problem Points
It is easy for stronger personalities to take advantage of Mice. Their inability to say 'no' and strong sense of duty towards others make it practically impossible for them to avoid unreasonable demands.

Mice are not necessarily liked for their helpful ways, and others often become annoyed at their non-committal hovering. Appreciation is therefore not always forthcoming for any good deeds the Mouse has done.

THE MOUSE'S INNER STATE

Inside, the Mouse is much more complex than is apparent from the outside. Inside, there is turmoil and upheaval, because somewhere in there is an 'I' that wants to come out, that has needs and urges that have been dutifully repressed for years.

A great need for appreciation and recognition drives the Mouse to more and more good deeds and selfless acts, and if this is not praised sufficiently by others, the Mouse becomes frustrated, and this drives him or her to even more selfless acts, sometimes virtually pursuing others to off-load good deeds on to them for a potential reward of recognition. If this is not forthcoming, the Mouse feels angry, but as anger is a forbidden feeling for an angel, it has to be suppressed and the little 'I' becomes even smaller. The Mouse is prone to exhaustion and nervous illnesses from suppressed feelings and wishes.

The Martyr

The Martyr (another mainly female trait of personality) will tell everyone how weak she is, when really, underneath it all, she is as strong as an ox. Martyrs have great stamina and determination and put all their energy into getting their own way and absolute attention from everyone around them because it is attention they feel they need, deserve and have a right to. They will dwell on how they unselfishly lent you a fiver three years ago and demand eternal gratitude for this generous act.

Although Martyrs seem to use others mainly as an audience, they are dependent on other people providing them with self-esteem. Attaining a sense of importance and self-respect through others is their main (unconscious or conscious) aim in life, and they make sure they get it. They are reasonably knowledgeable about illnesses and their symptoms and keep you posted at all times on their state of health, which, needless to say, is always poor or gives cause for worry.

Mothers sometimes employ this behaviour as emotional blackmail in order to prevent their only child from leaving the parental home for good or from going out in the evening and developing some sort of private life. The moment the daughter or son reaches for the door handle, up comes mother's hand over her heart, and, with a crooked but brave little smile, she'll wish her child a pleasant evening, but the message really is, 'Do go out, by all means! It doesn't matter if I have a heart attack while you're out having fun'. If the child is a Mouse, he or she will be unable to ignore these signals and stay at home.

The true challenge occurs when two Martyrs meet. The conversation will become very intense and quickly develop into a verbal duel about who is sicker, who has had the most severe illness and the greatest number of operations ('The surgeon couldn't *believe* how anyone can survive with a gallstone that size!'). Both are mostly speaking at the same time and not really listening to what the other person is saying because they are too busy trying to remember details of their illnesses in order to triumph over their opponent.

THE MARTYR'S GOOD POINTS
The Martyr has high levels of energy and determination. Unfortunately, they are misdirected.

THE MARTYR'S PROBLEM POINTS
The Martyr attracts the Mouse. It is like a sadist-masochist relationship: the Martyr moans, the Mouse listens in awe and feels needed.

Other people will tend to stay away from the Martyr because there is only so much lamentation you can take. When people stop coming to see Martyrs, they feel stranded with all their insecurity and proceed to produce more symptoms so that everyone begins to feel guilty and comes running back to their sick-bed, because this time they might *really* be ill …

Martyrs are in danger of developing very real illnesses, purely because they are thinking of them all the time (see pages 130–1).

THE MARTYR'S INNER STATE
Martyrs are really lonely and insecure people who have never had enough attention in their lives. Being ill has worked once to get attention, so they use it

over and over again. If they are lucky enough to come across someone who will not be blackmailed *and* is interested enough in them to show them different and more positive ways of gaining attention, they can learn to channel their energy into a more constructive direction and show surprising new qualities in their personality.

The Macho Man

These days, the Macho Man comes in many guises. He is by no means always that gift-wrapped stud that you might imagine. He can just as well be dressed with taste, carry a laptop and frequent the wine bar next to the office in the City.

Though an apparently uninhibited and outgoing person, the Macho Man has one taboo area – the truth about his own sexual performance, which usually leaves a lot to be desired. The Macho Man, however, will not let truth stand in the way of a good story, and he has lots of stories to tell, preferably in the company of other men or, sometimes, a few giggly girls.

His recent conquests will dominate the conversation, and he does not spare the listener details about how he did it, how many times and the name and address of the girl concerned. Alone with a woman, the Macho Man will still go on about other women, how he did it, how many times and the name and address of the girl concerned, which is not only extremely disruptive to any intimacy that might develop, it is also somewhat unpleasant for the woman he is with at the time.

All the talking is, consciously or unconsciously, designed to distract from his inability to perform adequately in bed, and very often the ploy works, as some women will begin to wonder whether it is maybe a shortcoming in them that causes this otherwise virile man to falter in bed with them.

Out of bed and on the motorway, the Macho Man displays more 'here-I-come' behaviour. In the fast lane, he will drive up close behind you at great speed and flash his lights at you when it is patently clear that there are two lorries on your left and three in front of you and there is no way you can let him pass. This tailgating is really nothing but an adult version of a little boy crying, 'Mummy, mummy, watch me!', the only difference being that now he has a car instead of a tricycle. The stage of maturity, though, is roughly the same as when he had the tricycle.

The Macho Man's Good Points
It is wonderful when he stops talking.

The Macho Man's Problem Points
The Macho Man mainly causes problems for others – especially the woman he is with at the time – because he cannot bear true intimacy. He lives on the surface of life and prefers relationships that do not make any demands on him.

The Macho Man is the hunting, haunted kind: hunting the next woman even before he has finished his present adventure, haunted by his own inability to become intimately involved in a relationship.

The Macho Man's Inner State
He is a lonely man whose immature behaviour covers up a badly damaged sense of self-esteem and great insecurity, often resulting from abuse and emotional neglect during his formative years. His inability or unwillingness to admit that anything is wrong makes it nearly impossible for him to seek help.

The Backstabber

There are male and female backstabbers, and they are not confined to the office environment. Backstabbing is a trait that is found in people with an inferiority complex who say 'yes' when they really want to say 'no', and who find themselves utterly unable to voice their opinion when they disagree with someone else, especially if they regard this other person as being of a higher rank than they are.

The Backstabber will be sweet as pie as long as they are speaking to another person, but as soon as he or she has left the room, backstabbing commences. The Backstabber's whole facial expression changes in a split-second from a bright, beaming smile to an angry or disdainful frown and then he or she either begins to gossip about the absent person or, at worst, to maliciously slander them.

Backstabbers use an indirect method of letting off steam when they feel that they are under someone else's thumb. It is an immensely destructive way of dealing with others because all backstabbing does is to poison the atmosphere and make the Backstabber more and more uptight, without actually doing anything about the problem.

Backstabbers in the office will accept more and more work from their superiors, although they know that they will not be able to cope with the workload. Backstabbers feel that they are being exploited and treated badly, and they resent it bitterly. Their solution to this problem it to go round and tell everyone in the office what a lousy boss they have. The only person who will never hear any complaints from the Backstabber is the only person who could do something to solve the problem – the boss.

THE BACKSTABBER'S GOOD POINTS
Lots of energy which, unfortunately, is misdirected.

THE BACKSTABBER'S PROBLEM POINTS
One Backstabber can often ruin the atmosphere for everyone else who works or lives with them. Backstabbers get themselves into a rut of resentment. Because they cannot make themselves address a problem directly, they feel less and less in control of what is happening to them, and this in turn gradually reduces to nothing the little self-confidence they may have had to start with, and so a vicious circle is established.

THE BACKSTABBER'S INNER STATE
Backstabbing can develop (it does not have to, though) when a person has been repeatedly punished for speaking their mind or for complaining. Again, this is most influential when it happens during childhood or adolescence, but it can also happen later in life when a person you live with puts you down continuously. Suppressing someone's right to speak out can result in that person feeling that they are worthless, or at least worth less than everyone else. They cannot express their anger and frustration, so they have to look for other ways of getting rid of bottled-up tension, and that can be by employing backstabbing.

The Workaholic

For some people, work is the ultimate four-letter-word. For the Workaholic, it is quite the opposite.

The Workaholic eats, sleeps and thinks work and couldn't stop it if he wanted to. Just like the Mouse, the Workaholic's behaviour is useful to others and therefore accepted as positive, although for the Workaholic, it is self-destructive. There are people who work hard, but that is not the same thing as being a Workaholic.

Workaholics have made work their only interest in life and, if there is nothing to do, they will create something to do. Workaholics are incapable of relaxing because they do not really want to relax. Relaxation to them is a waste of precious time when they could be working on that new contract.

Women Workaholics are often found in the middle echelons of companies, and they become Workaholics because of an inner pressure to have to be better than male colleagues in order to be accepted by them.

Workaholics will not be stopped by anything or anyone: while they are still in hospital recovering from a stress-induced heart attack, they already have arranged for a telephone by their bed and get a collaborator from the office to smuggle in the latest files '... on the Bramble and Lawson case, just so that I can stay on top of things'. They spend the first half of their lives ruining their health to make money, and then they spend the second half paying out that money to get their health back. It simply does not make sense, does it?

THE WORKAHOLIC'S GOOD POINTS
Workaholics are very conscientious people with a lot of drive who are highly motivated and have a great sense of responsibility and commitment.

THE WORKAHOLIC'S PROBLEM POINTS
Workaholics are not necessarily very efficient and they certainly do not control their work: their work controls them. (It is this point that gets Workaholics to co-operate with me when they come for stress management. As I know that they will not be impressed by the prediction that they might drop dead within the next half year if they carry on like that, I tell them that they will achieve a lot more if only they changed their ways, and they are wonderfully receptive to this idea and ready to get going!)

Relationships do not stand a chance in the life of Workaholics because they cannot bring themselves to allocate any of their waking time to non-work issues. Workaholics' health is bound to suffer considerably because they run down their bodies consistently without giving them a chance to recover.

The Workaholic's Inner State

Incessant working can be a sign of latent depression. Being perpetually busy prevents you from sitting down and allowing critical thoughts about yourself to come up. Other reasons for compulsive working can be a feeling of being inferior to colleagues, of being in a job that is two sizes too big for you, or it can be an escape route out of an unbearable situation at home.

Part

Three

8 How to Use This Par of The Book

▼ ▼ ▼ ▼

In this part of the book, you will find discussions on a few specific problems that participants of my courses or clients that come to see me individually mention again and again as being particularly aggravating.

At the beginning of each chapter, you will find a list of Statements that characterise that particular problem. Take the time to read through each point and decide whether it applies to you. There is no need to count how many Statements in the 'Loneliness' section are true for you. You are not more lonely if you 'score' ten points than if you score only one. The Statements are simply there to heighten your awareness of what reasons people think lie behind their feelings of loneliness.

The section following this list looks at each of the Statements in turn, examining what attitudes lie behind them and how you can learn to approach a problem from a different angle and think in a more positive way about it.

Following that, you will find Scripts that will help you establish the new constructive thought pattern in your subconscious mind. There is always a Script at the very end, but in some sub-sections there are additional Scripts to help you deal with that particular point.

It is essential that you read your Script several times a day. Copy it on to a piece of paper and carry it around with you. Learn it by heart and say it over and over again to yourself, plant it firmly into your subconscious mind by constant repetition.

As the Scripts contain only positive thoughts, you will also feel a beneficial physical effect. As you think pleasant, constructive thoughts, your body relaxes. If you doubt this, just try to do the opposite. Recall a past experience where you got very angry. Bring it back into your mind for a moment. You will notice how your body reacts to these negative thoughts: your jaw muscles tighten up, you tense up around the stomach area, your blood-pressure goes up, which produces a feeling of pressure in your head, and you are generally feeling very uncomfortable.

Luckily, the system works just as well the other way round. When you fill your mind with positive memories or thoughts, your body releases tension, your muscles and organs relax and work together in harmony, and a sense of well-being pervades your body. To enhance the effect of the Scripts, spend some time in the evening relaxing and visualising the positive solution to your particular problem.

Don't waste any more time thinking about the problem, spend time thinking about the successful outcome. For every hold-up you encounter on your way, for every obstacle that bars your way to success, you will find two new possible ways of dealing with it. If one door closes, another two doors open. Don't spend time looking at the wall, look for the doors in the wall. Be constructive in the way you are dealing with problems. It happens very often that people cannot imagine how their particular problem could possibly be solved and you despair, get frantic or lose all hope and get very depressed.

Think back. This is not the first time you have had a problem. What happened last time? Suddenly, out of the blue, a solution appeared, and I bet you anything that it was a solution you had never dreamed of. It makes a lot more sense to calm down, relax and *believe* that a solution will present itself at the right moment in time than to make yourself unhappy worrying about the problem.

Although we solve problems day in and day out we still lack the belief that the next problem is going to be solved. Our rational mind is far too restricted to anticipate the solution that we end up with. Let's stop over-estimating our brains, they are not as wonderfully competent as our IQ makes us believe. A person who boasts about their high IQ is like a prisoner who boasts about his big cell.

Intuition, which originates in the subconscious mind, is far more efficient at solving our problems. Pay attention to your dreams and intuitive thoughts, and you will often find that they show you the way to the solution of a problem. Solving problems has nothing to do with hard work, it is child's play, born out of a relaxed attitude. The greatest ideas, the most ingenious inventions were made by 'accident' while the person was not even thinking about the problem. Albert Einstein said that when he was trying to solve a mathematical problem he formulated the problem precisely in his mind and then stopped thinking about it. The answer would invariably come up after a while, spontaneously. The subconscious mind works for us all the time, even while we are asleep, and produces the answers and solutions we need.

Finally, you will find a Short Form, a type of mini-Script, that should be used during the night. If something bothers you during the day, you can wake up in the middle of the night and start thinking about it. At night, problems tend to become blown out of all proportion, monopolising your head, spiralling round and round endlessly, so that you find it impossible to go back to sleep.

The Short Form can be easily remembered and should be repeated in a mechanical way in your mind as you are lying in bed. Again, the positive content of the Short Form helps to relax your body, which is what you need to be able to go back to sleep. As there is nothing you can do in the middle of the night to solve your problem you might as well postpone thinking about it until the next day.

9 | Communication

▼ ▼ ▼ ▼

- I hate arguments.
- I find it difficult to tell others what I want.
- When I feel hurt, I sulk.

Communication occurs on many levels and in various forms. It surrounds us everywhere, in letters, advertisements, films, on the radio. Messages are sent to us perpetually, and we respond to them. Communication enables us to stay in touch with the world around us and to send out and receive messages from other people.

Communication is immensely complex. Not only do we stay in touch with others by speaking and writing to them, we also express ourselves by using physical sign language. Even when we refuse to communicate we give a message to others.

Communication is vital to the development and maintenance of relationships. As relationships change over time, it becomes necessary to adjust to altered circumstances and inform others about our intentions and wishes. In order to make relationships satisfactory and effective, we need to learn about others and, at the same time, give out information about ourselves. We cannot expect other people to read our minds. It is up to us to let them know about our wishes and expectations.

Information does not have to be passed on verbally. The raising of the eyebrows can indicate to your partner that you doubt what he has just said or that you are amazed at the information received.

Physical language has many facets to it. A slight change in the tone of your voice, your facial expression, a tiny movement or change in posture that accompanies something you say can add extra information to its content. Body language can emphasise or tone down; it can convey that you are only joking or that you are giving away a secret. Through it we communicate much more than just words. When somebody does not maintain eye contact as he speaks to you, this has a number of effects. You may think he is shy and therefore you make an effort to put him at ease or you may think he is conceited, which annoys you and so you keep your replies to a minimum. You can see how easily mis-communication can occur: if you thought he was conceited when he was only shy your response would have been totally inappropriate, even more so if he had been blind.

Whether you assume that the other person is shy or conceited will depend on your expectations, and your expectations result from your past experience. Equally, if your partner speaks to you in a certain way and is unable to look at you, this reflects his or her expectations of you. Your partner could be afraid that you might be bossy or look down on him or her, so avoids eye contact to prevent any acts of aggression on your part.

Communication is a two-way process. The sender and receiver interact with one another constantly so that everyone is a sender and a receiver at the same time. While you are speaking to someone, you simultaneously monitor his or her response, and this may well influence how you continue. When you see your partner frown as you are telling her about an incident at the office you may decide not to mention another event so as not to upset her further. If she is upset, *you* get upset, so you protect your own peace of mind by discontinuing the conversation.

Another factor that will determine how you communicate is the environment. You adopt different roles depending on who you are speaking to and where the conversation takes place. A woman will adopt a particular way of speaking when she acts as 'mother', and an entirely different one when she adopts her role of 'boss' at work. A man will express himself in one way when he is discussing business with a colleague and another way when he is speaking about his job to a friend at a party.

As we are all required to adopt a number of different roles throughout life, our way of communicating has to be flexible. With each new role – as student, parent, spouse, employee – we have to learn the appropriate language, the appropriate means of communicating within that new context. How adaptable we are in taking on new roles is largely dependent on previous experience. Our communication skills are derived from what we have learnt as children from our parents. Previous learning governs how we communicate with others, how communication patterns develop and how they are maintained in our relationships.

Communication is very complex and it is therefore not surprising that errors occur. Feelings play a powerful role in our ability to convey messages to others. Some situations may leave us virtually speechless, others make us react defiantly so that we break off communication temporarily.

The most drastic examples of being cut off from the outside world are to be found in schizophrenia and severe depression. When the world appears to be a menacing place and a person cannot see a way of escaping his problems or defending himself against the demands that come from the environment, then his situation may appear to be such a massive threat to him that the subconscious mind erects a defence barrier against the outside world. It just cuts the person off, preventing the outside world from having access and hurting him any more.

Part of this defence mechanism can be to build up an internal world that has its own language – its own meanings and symbols that cannot be understood by other people. It is like a new mind-language, a different way of thinking about the world that separates the schizophrenic from his or her environment.

In severe depression, a person will still be in touch with reality mentally, but will make every effort to avoid contact with others. Anything new, anything outside his or her routine is experienced as frightening, so the depressed person will withdraw from it as soon as possible. The only safe place in the world is bed, where he can just pull the blanket over his head and draw mental curtains shutting out the world. It is like an escape back into the womb where you are being fed and where it is safe and warm without having to do anything, without having to think or act, where you can just 'be' without conflicts or hassles.

Both schizophrenic and depressive illnesses, just like any other illnesses, carry a message. The disrupted flow of communication informs the environment that there is an imbalance in the relational system that needs to be redressed. Mental illnesses occur for a reason, they don't descend on people out of the blue. Where there is a symptom there is also a cause.

In every family there are specific rules about communication. These are not rules that anyone officially set out. It is just understood that there are certain topics that must not be touched upon (such as sex or a relative who the family has fallen out with), certain feelings that must not be expressed (such as anger). There may also be double standards where there is one set of rules for adults and another for children, or one set of rules for the father, another one for the mother and the children, or one set of rules for the sick child and another for the healthy siblings. Adults may be allowed to tell lies while the children are punished for it. It may be acceptable when the father does not lift a finger in the house, but the rest of the family are called 'lazy' when they don't help. The sick child may get away with being naughty while his siblings incur punishment when they don't behave.

These rules translate into meanings, each family member translating them in their own way. Let us assume there is an asthmatic child in the family. The doctor tells the parents that the child must not be upset because that might trigger an attack – rule number 1. There is also the parental rule that the children are not allowed to bounce about on the sofa – rule number 2.

When the occasion arises where the asthmatic child bounces on the sofa, the parents find themselves in a dilemma. They want to maintain their own rule, but they do not want to endanger the child's health. The reasoning will be, 'If we tell him off he is going to get upset and then he might have an attack. We will just have to suppress our anger and let him do it. We cannot really stop his behaviour without causing him harm.' The sisters and brothers are angry with the parents and jealous of the asthmatic child, saying, 'This is not fair. He is allowed everything just because he is ill. I can't help it that I'm not ill. I want just as much attention and freedom.' And the asthmatic child thinks, 'It's not so bad being ill after all. I'm getting all the attention and I can get away with anything. It's really easy to manipulate my parents. Let's do it some more!'

The conflicting rules compromise the parents' position in the family and make them vulnerable to blackmail. The other children feel that they are permanently playing second fiddle to the sick brother and see their parents as weak and unfair for giving in to him. Nothing these other children do to attract attention, be it in a good or bad way, will ever be enough to outdo the sick child. A frustrating thought indeed.

Conflicting rules create problems all around, even for the sick child. As the illness brings so many advantages there is hardly any incentive for getting better. Illness seems a small price to pay for the attention it brings.

Other problems can arise from ambiguous communication. This occurs when a person says one thing but expresses the contrary through body language. A mother may, for example, feel bothered by her child, but instead of saying, 'Leave me alone, I'm sick of you', she says, 'Go to bed. You look tired and I want you to get some sleep'. If the child accepts the mother's loving concern at face value, he may draw closer to her, but that is, of course, just the opposite of what she wants and she will probably get cross with him. This would leave the child confused. He would not understand what he has done to evoke his mother's anger. If he accused his mother of being contradictory, she might react in a hurt way, making him feel guilty, so that does not really get him off the hook.

The mother, on the other hand, may feel that it is impossible to tell her child to leave her alone because this would go against her idea of what a good mother should feel. She wants to be a good mother so she cannot possibly let on that she is fed up with the child – but she is, and her reactions give her away in the end.

I hate arguments

Some people will do anything to avoid arguments. They experience arguments as so traumatic that they may even feel sick when they are faced with one. Even just listening to other people arguing can make them react with fear or unpleasant physical sensations. These can be headaches, nausea, rising blood-pressure, palpitations or just a general sense of being unwell. These symptoms become particularly strong when you cannot leave the scene, when you are in a car with the people who are having the argument, for example.

When arguments have such a strong, negative effect on you then it is more than likely that you have witnessed quite a few arguments as a child and that they have frightened you very much.

Try and look at arguments from a child's point of view. Her parents are fighting, they are yelling at one another, maybe saying things they don't really mean. As they are screaming at each other they look like they hate one another (and they certainly do at that moment). The child witnesses this scene with horror. There is a lot of noise going on and the two most important people in her life are fighting. Are they going to hurt one another? Everything is in uproar. Why are they screaming? Is it something the child has done? If the child wasn't there, maybe the parents would not have to fight over money? If the child wasn't there, maybe the mother would be happier because she could go out more? Some parents will openly accuse the child for the difficulties they are in, but even without that happening, children will often blame themselves.

A child is totally and utterly dependent on its parents, in every respect. It relies on the parents for food, clothes, shelter, love and security. It relies on them for the fulfilment of all its needs, so when the family unit is jeopardised in any way, the child feels threatened in its very existence.

When rows occur regularly, they can leave a child with a profound sense of insecurity and, consequently, it will do anything to appease the parents or distract their attention. Illness can be one (subconscious) means of achieving this. If the child is ill the parents have to concentrate on the child for a while and postpone the settling of differences.

Another way children deal with their feelings of insecurity and guilt is that they become delinquent. This provides distraction and aligns their actions with their feelings. Since they feel guilty anyway they might as well do something to feel guilty about. It may be wrong to steal, but at least you know why you feel guilty.

You can also be afraid of rows because you have never been allowed to raise your voice. Maybe it was not a done thing in your family to utter grievances openly. Instead, the 'culprit' may have been punished by silence. In some families it is customary to stop speaking to someone who you feel has done you wrong. For a child, this form of punishment is very harsh. To be ignored is to be rejected, and to be rejected when you are in a vulnerable position is very hurtful.

Even though many years may have passed since then, you can still carry these feelings of anxiety, guilt and rejection. Your fear of arguments could go back a long time. Look at your past. Ask your sisters and brothers or other relatives to help you remember. Once you can identify the cause of your fear, you will find it easier to deal with it.

Become aware of the fact that you are no longer that child, that you are grown up, that your situation has changed. Those fears belong to a time that has gone. You are able to set new rules now. When people argue, they do not argue because of you.

When someone is irritable with you, there is no need for you to feel guilty. You understand now that people have their own reasons for being in a bad mood or for being discontented, *but in 99 per cent of the cases it is not you.* Begin to concentrate on that 99 per cent instead of the 1 per cent. Make it your own private new rule that you are innocent until proven guilty.

If you adopt this new rule you can also allow yourself to widen your action radius. As you have decided not to feel guilty any more, you can adopt new strategies in arguments. All of a sudden you have new options. You may begin to listen with interest rather than with fear when others argue. You may want to listen carefully and examine what your opinion is. Who do you think is right? (Whatever your decision is, keep it to yourself!) Make out that you are a journalist who is witnessing an important event and has to report it to his paper later on. You can speak quite normally to the couple once they have had their argument because you have nothing to do with it.

When someone is shouting at you, rather than appeasing them at all costs, you may declare that you refuse to talk with them unless they calm down. Then you can just put down the receiver or walk out of the room.

Once you stop being afraid of arguments you will find that your social position becomes stronger. You have more power and influence because you do not feel you have to accept it when people try to bully you, overload you with work or when they make unreasonable demands.

As you are no longer afraid of arguments you can take the risk of provoking a row with your more self-assured attitude. People will feel that change in you, and I promise you that you will encounter far less unpleasantness than you did when you were so very obliging, doing everything to avoid a row.

SCRIPT

I am all right. I have not made any more mistakes than anyone else. I am a worthy member of society. I now leave guilt and fear behind me. Other people are responsible for their own moods and feelings, I am responsible for mine. I am calm and collected at all times. I am sure of my own worth and other people can feel that.

Arguments are just differences of opinion. This is a normal thing to occur. I am entitled to speak my mind and so is everyone else.I speak my mind calmly and state my needs clearly. Others listen to me. A solution can always be found. I am good at negotiating for myself. I am strong and confident.

SHORT FORM

• Arguments are OK. They just signify a difference of opinion. I stay calm and relaxed.

I find it difficult to tell others what I want

What is holding you back? Do you find it difficult to convey your wishes to others or is it that you don't really know what it is you want? You may even find that you have problems with both these aspects.

When you are a young child it is a straightforward matter to say what you want. As a baby, all you have to do is cry and, with a bit of luck, someone comes running with food or checks whether you need a new nappy. Even a bit later on, the direct approach works quite well. You point your finger at something and say 'doll' or 'teddy' and an enraptured auntie passes you whatever you were after. You may have to make minor concessions a few months later when your mother begins to insist you say 'please' and 'thank you' to get what you want, but that is still OK.

The enthusiasm about your ability to speak your first words soon wears off, however, and the flow of your demands is curbed more and more. You are told to hold back, to restrain yourself, you are told that it is impolite to speak out. Children should be seen, not heard. You are told that children should be grateful for what they get, that to want more is greedy. Society is beginning to take its toll. Individualism can become disruptive within a group of people such as the family, so the new member of society is instructed to adapt to the group.

This can be a bit of a struggle because the child is asked to give up quite a few of its privileges. Once you could burp, and the whole family applauded. Only a few years later, you are 'disgusting' when you do the same thing. Once you could stare at people, now you are 'rude' when you do it. Once you could run around naked, now you are told off for doing so. What has been 'sweet' so far is now naughty or impolite. Things that were encouraged once are now prohibited or even punished. It is a bit like having all the perks taken away from your job and having them replaced by a number of chores that were never in your job description when you started. It is not really surprising that children don't like it.

We all have to go through this process and cope with the restrictions it brings. A problem only arises when conformity is forced on you in such a way that you feel you can no longer be yourself. When you have been made to feel guilty about speaking your mind or contradicting your parents ('You are ungrateful!'), you come to regard your own opinion as secondary and the consequences of speaking out as unpleasant. Not only does it earn you your parents' disapproval, it also makes you feel uncomfortable emotionally because you have learnt by now that you do not contradict your parents or superiors. Even when you finally leave home, you still carry your parents' admonitions with you in your head. This phenomenon is commonly known as 'conscience' and it works on a subconscious level, which makes it more difficult to switch it off.

This learnt automatic response of not speaking out to avoid unpleasant emotional sensations is convenient for others because it means that they can get on with what they are doing without being interrupted by someone who may criticise them. This is why timidity is often praised as 'good manners' when really it is to the disadvantage of the shy person.

When a shy person feels very strongly about something but feels too inhibited to speak about it, this can create great inner conflict. The emotion implodes rather than explodes, and if this happens over a long period of time, mental or physical problems can be the consequence.

If you have been told from an early age that your wishes are secondary, or even impudent, you come to suppress them. You begin to think in 'oughts' and 'shoulds' and begin to disregard your own wishes yourself. But that does not make them go away, it just makes you feel confused. You can feel that you are discontent, but you cannot understand why.

To rediscover your own needs, think about your present situation. What are the things you would like to change if you had a magic wand? Look at all the things you feel unhappy about. Check the state of your relationship with others, your work situation, your health, your overall well-being. Without taking into account whether you think changes can be achieved, imagine how things would be ideally. Here you have it. That is what you want!

Don't be frightened by the boldness of your imagination. You will probably have to do some more work on your self-confidence before you can realise your ambitions, but at least you know what you are aiming for.

Now to the second part of the problem of expressing to others what you want. Maybe it has been drummed into your head that you must not ask for things but wait until they are given to you. This procedure works admirably when it comes to your telephone bill. Indeed there is no need to ask for it because you will get it anyway. And even if you lose it they are going to send you a second one. So far so good. The moment you want some money from someone else, however, the system fails to work. Just sitting at home hoping for your bank, a friend or the tooth fairy to ring and *offer* you the money is unlikely to produce results. Just *hoping* that your boss will give you more interesting work one day will only lead to harsh disappointment. Unless you say something, nothing is going to happen.

The only chance of getting what you want is to speak about it. After all, your telephone bill asks you for *your* money, doesn't it? And your parents told you when they wanted you to do something, so it cannot be that wrong. You are an adult now, so you have the same right that your parents had then.

You don't have to be loud or impolite or aggressive when you utter your wishes. You can be pleasant and speak in a quiet voice and still get what you want. Try it on smaller things first. Ask someone in the street for directions or for the right time. Do it a few times until you feel comfortable with it, then work your way up to more difficult things. Ask a colleague at work to mind your phone while you are out. Tell your boss that you want to leave on time tonight. Tell your children that you expect them to do little chores around the house from now on.

It is a lot better to say what you want than to stew over the thought that everyone gets what *they* want except you. You will feel more in control of your life simply because you know that you can get what you need for yourself.

SCRIPT

It is OK to want things. I have the right to want things for myself. I stand up for myself. I insist on having some of my needs fulfilled, and I am doing this in a pleasant way.

I understand that other people cannot read my mind and that it is up to me to inform them about my wishes. I make sure that I keep a reasonable balance between giving and taking. I have a responsibility towards myself. My happiness is important to me.

SHORT FORM

- **I make sure that others know about my wishes. I do this in a pleasant way.**

When I feel hurt I sulk

Sulking is a way of disrupting communication in order to punish others for not giving you what you want. The underlying attitude is that of a person who thinks she should have whatever she wants at once, without having to ask for it – or, at least, without having to ask for it more than once.

Sulking is a habit that runs in entire families, sometimes over generations. It is closely connected with obstinacy and can seriously disturb relationships within the family. Often, the incident that provokes the sulking bout is trivial, but the punishment is severe. There are families where various members have not spoken to one another for years, sometimes decades. No one can really remember what the reason for this super-sulk was, but it must have been a good one – after all you have not spoken to Uncle Harry for 15 years …

The longer the sulking goes on, the more difficult it becomes to put an end to it. It is seen as a sign of weakness to be the first one to start speaking to the other party again. It would be like admitting that you were wrong 15 years ago, and that is the last thing you want to do. The situation has come to a deadlock.

On a less extreme level, sulking can be your way of stamping your foot when you feel left out: when you don't get all the attention, you sulk; when someone else gets the job you were interested in, you sulk; when your birthday present is not big enough, you sulk. You feel you have an automatic right to anything you may want, but you are not really prepared to work for it. You are deftly bypassing this strenuous part of the process.

Once a thought has settled in your mind, you want your wish to be fulfilled in just the way you imagined it. The basic concept is good, it is just the method that does not work. It is good to be sure about what it is you want – it is great that you know you want a new job – but it is childish to insist on that *particular* job and feel hurt when you don't get it.

Stop clamouring for justice. You may well have been the better person for the job, but you did not get it because you are a woman. This admittedly is unfair, but there is nothing you can do about it. At this stage you have two options: you can sit and sulk and brood over the injustice of life and injustice to you in particular, or you can apply for another job. If you are serious about wanting another job then I strongly suggest you go for the second option.

Note: Never give up.

There are no guarantees in life, there are only opportunities, and there are always more opportunities where the last one came from. Be flexible, be open to the different jobs that are on offer. If you did not get this one it only means that a better job is on its way.

Another situation that brings out the sulks is lack of attention. Say your husband or wife has started a new job and has become really involved in it, so much so that he or she does not seem to have any time for you. Although you are happy and proud that your partner is doing so well, you also feel that their enthusiasm for the job deprives you of attention, but, instead of saying that you feel left out, you sulk. When he or she asks you what the matter is you won't say. Your partner may then think that you have had problems at work and get angry at you for taking it out on them.

When you are angry or hurt about something your partner does and you sulk, then you are withholding your love. Sulking is a form of revenge or punishment that pushes the other person away from you and ultimately destroys trust and intimacy. It is a negative form of reaction that does not get you or anyone else anywhere.

The main point about sulking is that it does not accomplish anything. It does not get you what you want, namely loving attention. To get what you want you have to ask for it, so don't let the self-pity squad come to get you. It is up to you to explain what it is you need.

Note: Other people cannot read your mind.

You are not happy when you are sulking, others are not happy when you are sulking, so why go on with it? You will have a far better time without it and you will increase your chances of getting what you want.

Script

It is a good thing that I know what I want. I approach my aims with confidence. I am fully awake to the opportunities that come my way and this helps me reach my goal. Any problems I encounter on the way I deal with efficiently and calmly. Setbacks on the way help me to find new ways. My needs are important to me and I find it easy to communicate them in a nice manner to others. I stay flexible and reach for my goals with confidence.

SHORT FORM

- My needs are important to me. I help others to help me get what I need.
  or
- I pursue goals with confidence.

10 | Stress

▼ ▼ ▼ ▼

- I feel I cannot cope with my workload.
- If I make the slightest mistake, I feel I have to do the job again.
- It takes me a long time to switch off from work when I get home.
- I am constantly irritable, aggressive or tearful.
- Any sense of relaxation after a holiday is gone the moment I step into the office on the first day back.
- I have had sexual problems since I started feeling so stressed.
- I have just had a heart attack.
- I don't have time for breaks.

Stress is not a privilege of the upper ranks of management, it cuts across all levels of society. We all have to deal with the ups and downs of everyday life, adjusting constantly to new situations.

As long as we feel we are on top of it all, we are OK. It is when we begin to feel out of control, when we feel we are not up to the task ahead of us that we display symptoms of stress. For example, your son could be a nervous wreck and totally exhausted after only half an hour of revising French grammar, but he could sit up all night trying to sort out a problem on the computer without showing the slightest sign of fatigue or irritation. Whether you react positively or negatively to stress depends very much on whether you consider your work a challenge or a nuisance.

The human body is very well equipped for these constant adaptation processes that we are confronted with every day. Our brain helps us perceive a situation as difficult or potentially dangerous and sends a signal down to the nervous system, which, in turn, immediately adjusts our physical functions to provide an increase in energy to help us deal more efficiently with the task ahead. To take an example, if your house is on fire, your brain (via your eyes) registers the flames and immediately sends an alarm signal to your sympathetic nervous system. As a consequence, adrenalin is pumped into the bloodstream, your heart rate goes up, your blood-pressure goes up, blood sugar is released, you tense your muscles, your breathing becomes shallow and you start running out of the house. All this happens in a split second. In the circumstances this is a useful reaction and will probably save your life. If, however, you react in this way when you are trying to take your driving test or to make a speech, it is a nuisance because your normal thinking is blocked.

Physical stress reactions are very old survival mechanisms. In order to escape a herd of stampeding bisons it was necessary for primitive man to start running *immediately*, without thinking about it. The physical state of panic he was in prevented him from considering whether he should nip back into his hut to get his club out or not. Rational thinking was virtually switched off because any hesitation would have slowed him down and jeopardised his survival.

These days we rarely face situations of real physical danger where we need to make use of this 'fight or flight' mechanism, but the mechanism still operates nonetheless. What helped primitive man to save his skin has now become an unsuitable response. These days it is the individual who reacts slowest to stressful situations who survives. We are no longer surrounded by life-threatening animals and most of us don't have to struggle for basic needs like food and shelter, so we can afford to shift our 'danger' label to other, more contemporary things like job insecurity, tests and exams and work overload.

One very important point to note is that it is not the situation as such that produces the stress; it is your *attitude* towards that situation that will decide whether you react with stress or not. If, for example, you regard your exam as a threat, you are less likely to do well in it than someone who regards the exam as a challenge.

Stress is not integral to the situation. If it were, then some people could not go into an exam in a calm and relaxed manner, while others freaked out and were unable to think clearly – they would all react in the same way to the exam situation. The *situation* is the same for those who react calmly to the exam situation and for those who are panicked by it, they just *perceive* it in different ways. A heavy workload is therefore not the same thing as being under stress, and just because you have a lot of responsibility does *not* mean that you will automatically develop an ulcer and suffer from insomnia.

Body and brain work closely together. Whatever messages the brain (rational mind) sends down from the command bridge will be carried out by the crew (nervous system). If the brain tells the nervous system that it has to cope with excessive demand, the sympathetic nervous system switches into overdrive. This happens like a chain reaction within a split second. If this capacity to adapt is exploited over a long period of time, the system breaks down. You end up with heart disease, a nervous breakdown or an ulcer, but, long before this happens, your body will warn you. Physical symptoms to heed are the following:

- breathlessness, dizziness, nausea
- over-eating or loss of appetite
- excessive smoking or drinking
- sleeping problems
- sexual problems
- sweating
- fidgeting and nail-biting
- head-, back- or neckaches

Mental symptoms that indicate stress problems are:

- deteriorating memory
- feelings of frustration/aggression/tearfulness
- indecisiveness
- feelings of being a failure
- lack of concentration
- depression
- anxiety

If you have a problem and react with stress to it, then you will display some of these physical and mental symptoms. If you have sleeping problems and feel depressed you are less likely to solve the problem that initiated the stress reaction, and that will exacerbate the situation. Because you cannot concentrate, you cannot solve the problem; consequently, you feel like a failure. That depresses you even more and you can concentrate even less. To break this vicious circle try the following.

First Aid

- Withdraw as soon as possible and sit down somewhere.
- Take a deep breath and close your eyes as you breathe out.
- Take another deep breath (always through your belly) and unclench your teeth.
- Take another deep breath and drop your shoulders.
- Take another deep breath and open your hands.
- Breathe in deeply, hold your breath for a count of five and breathe out again. Repeat this last step at least five times.

This First Aid exercise will help take the edge off the symptoms. It enables you to think clearly simply because you calm down and permit oxygen to reach the brain again.

When you are stressed you tighten up all the muscles and organs in your body, including your breathing apparatus. This results in shallow breathing and therefore less oxygen intake, which reduces your brain's level of activity.

Now to the specific points.

I feel I cannot cope with my workload

Let me emphasise first of all that just because you work from 7 a.m. to 9 p.m. without a break does not mean that you are good at what you are doing. Do not confuse *quantity* with *quality*. If you cannot cope with your workload within the limits of a reasonable working day then something is wrong somewhere.

What are you trying to prove by staying late all the time? That you are indispensable and that the company would collapse if it was not for your efforts? Don't kid yourself.

Are you still trying to prove to your parents that you can do it, that you are 'good'? Are you still seeking their approval and their praise? Because you don't get it, you work even harder. You are getting exhausted and make mistakes that you have to rectify, and that takes up even more time.

The above are broad questions that you should ask yourself at some stage. But let us look at the nitty-gritty problems now.

If you feel that you cannot cope with your workload, is this because you are disorganised? Are you one of those people who has a desk strewn with papers so that it takes half an hour of intensive digging to find the minutes of last month's board meeting?

You may laugh, but this is nothing to be proud of. An untidy desk reflects your state of mind: chaos inside equals chaos outside. Get organised and *stay* organised. This is up to you, not your secretary. Tidy up, file papers away.

Make it a rule that you never touch any paper twice. In other words, if you pick up a letter to file it away and you don't know where it goes, hold on to it and find out where the appropriate file is. Do not pick up any other papers until that letter is in its proper place.

Get your priorities right. Don't try and do three things at once. You cannot dictate a letter on to a tape, take a phonecall *and* tidy up your desk at the same time.

When you get into the office in the morning, do not make a beeline for the in-tray.

The first thing you do when you get in is to take your coat off and sit down. Don't do anything for a moment. Take a deep breath. Take a sheet of paper and start making a list of everything you have to do today and in the near future. Once you have done that, mark the things that have to be done today.

Before you start on any of the items, see whether you can delegate any tasks. Of the remaining items, start with the ones you like *least*. Get them out of the way first. Your energy level is highest in the morning. After lunch, your body and mind slow down considerably, making you less productive. It is also advantageous from a psychological point of view because you feel really good for the rest of the day for having finally tackled the unpleasant things rather than postponed them again.

If, by the end of the day, you have not been able to get everything on your 'today – urgent' list done *and* if this happens regularly you may want to consider the following.

Are you the company or family mule? Does everything land on your desk or in your hands because others won't do it? It is irrelevant in this context whether you are the boss or the secretary, the mother or the father.

If other people are using you to get rid of their junk you have to stop them. They must be told that you are not willing to put up with this any longer. *Do not* promise to meet deadlines that you know you cannot meet. *Do not* accept more work when you are snowed under already. Here are a couple of examples of how to deal with difficult situations.

The boss comes rushing in with a pile of handwritten papers. The secretary's in-tray is spilling over and she has been typing since 8.30 a.m. to get on top of her work. She is currently working on an important forecast paper that has to be finished by 10 a.m. the next morning.

Boss (in a rush): 'Here are the minutes. Make sure they are ready by tomorrow lunch-time!' (On his way out again.)
Secretary (in a clear voice): 'I'm afraid that won't be possible.'
Boss (turns around, irritated): 'Well, I need it. You'll just have to stay late.'
Secretary: 'I'm sorry but there is only so much I can do. I can tell you now that there is no way this will be ready by tomorrow lunch-time.'
Boss (exasperated): 'I don't care how you do it, just do it.'
Secretary: 'If you need it that urgently then I suggest we get a temp in first thing tomorrow morning. That is the only way it can be done.'
Boss: 'Get a temp in, get Santa Claus in, I don't care, as long as it gets done by tomorrow.'
(Exit boss, slamming door.)

Do not apologise for not being able to do it. It is important that you do not go into lengthy explanations why another piece of work has priority. Also, do not be blackmailed by your boss's bad mood. His bad mood is his problem, not yours. He was ratty when he came in, so you are not the cause of it. Make sure, too, that you keep repeating that what is asked of you cannot be done and keep repeating it until another solution has been found.

To take another example, imagine an elderly mother, eagerly awaiting her son's return from work. Finally, a key turns in the lock and he comes in, exhausted. He drops into the nearest chair.

Mother: 'Gerald, can you please take the dustbin outside?'
Son: 'Sure, just let me catch my breath. I'll do it in a minute. I'm totally shattered.'
(Pause, then)
Mother: 'Oh well, I suppose I'll have to do it myself then. Not that it does my back any good ...'
Son (remains seated): 'Well, mother, if you'd rather do your back in again than wait ten minutes, then I'm afraid I can't help you.
Mother (doesn't know what to say first. Then): 'You're ungrateful. After all that I've done for you. . .
Son (still not getting up): 'Don't worry, mother, I will take the bin out in a moment.'
(Mother grumbles and leaves the room.)

N.B.   *Do not be distracted by comments that contain blackmail messages such as, 'After all that I've done for you'. They have nothing to do with what you are discussing.*
N.B.   *Be adamant that you will not be hassled.*
N.B.   *Stay polite.*
N.B.   *Repeat your point until it has sunk in.*

You can say 'no' quite clearly without being aggressive or impolite. It is the simple repetition of your message that does the trick. Do not be lured away from your point by accusations or emotional blackmail. Persist and you will get what you want.

Once you have done this a few times other people begin to understand that you are not willing to accept extra work or to be ordered about and, after a short while, you will notice that people stop making unreasonable demands on you. You have become an assertive person and others will respect you for it.

If I make the slightest mistake, I feel I have to do the job again

If you are writing a letter and you mis-spell a word so that you have to cross it out, do you rip up the letter? If you have just hoovered in the living room and someone walks across the rug, do you go and straighten out the edges?

Do you find it unacceptable if others are not perfect? Then you must also find it unbearable that you yourself have faults and make mistakes. Whether you are at home or in the office, this means that you get so caught up in getting minor details right that you forget what you set out to do.

When you have to make two urgent phonecalls and dictate three important letters you will get hopelessly behind in your work schedule if you spend too much time trying to decide whether you like the layout of the letter your secretary has just typed for you. If you have lots to do at home you squander valuable energy if you keep wiping the work surface in the kitchen every time a family member breathes on it.

Get your priorities right. You will never be able to control everything and everyone around you, and your own performance is also subject to fluctuations. No one is perfect all the time – we all make mistakes, *this is normal.* You are by no means inferior to others just because you sometimes make mistakes.

If you think back, you will probably find that it was very hard to please one or both of your parents when you were young. You may have adored your mother, say, but whatever you did was never quite good enough to gain her approval. Maybe you were loved *only* when you complied with all the parental rules.

Children need to feel loved, so they will try everything to get this love. This can become a frustrating catch-22 situation where, as hard as you try, you can never quite get that love because you never quite manage to follow *all* the rules.

There is no need to continue this game later on in life, though – you deserve better than that. Make a list with all the things you like about yourself. Take your time over it, add to it whenever you think of additional points. Have you got a good sense of humour, are you considerate, a good listener, are you entertaining, are you a loyal friend, a caring person? Write it all down. Look at your list every day. That's you!

Begin to treat yourself as the nice person that you are. Don't go on making unreasonable demands on yourself. Give yourself a break. Ease up on all the rules you had set up for you when you were little. These rules are old and need revising. Circumstances have changed, you are no longer living with your parents. It is time you made your own rules, rules that suit you. You will see that being lenient with yourself helps you to work better and with less stress, simply because you are more relaxed.

> ### Note: You are your own best friend. Be kind to yourself.

It takes me a long time to switch off from work when I get home

You have already entered the stress spiral. This situation is only acceptable if it is for a limited period of time. While you are going through a stressful period, you need to make sure that you keep your weekends free. If you cannot do that, go in late in the morning or go home early whenever you can. Make sure, too, that you take a holiday after you have finished that particular job, *before* another urgent job comes up. Say it loud and clear that you will be away. Announce it as soon as you know when you can go. If something urgent comes up, they will find someone else to do it while you are away.

Don't carry the company's or the world's worries on your shoulders. You will only break your back, and then you are no good to anyone. Don't give in to the illusion that you are irreplaceable. If your company or your family want you to do a good job for them they have to allow you reasonable time off to recharge your batteries.

Your children have to learn that you are not a servant. You will have to teach them that, after they have reached a certain age, they are expected to take over certain tasks and that you are not there to wait on them hand and foot. Insist on having time to yourself, even if it is only half an hour a day. It gets your family used to the idea and later on you can easily extend that private time.

A change of scenery is often a good way of switching off. This can take the form of going away for the weekend, seeing some friends or pursuing a pastime or new activity. As a rule of thumb it is advisable to tailor your after-work activities to the amount of stress you are under. The higher your stress level at work, the less exhausting your pastime should be. It is nonsense to go from a stressful work environment to a stressful game of squash or a tiring weekend. What you need is distraction, not destruction. Even though you may have been sitting behind your desk all day without getting a lot of exercise this does not mean you are physically as fresh as a daisy.

Mental stress, as we have seen, has physical consequences. When you are under great pressure at work then this affects your body just as much as if you had just taken part in some strenuous physical exercise. This is why it is not a good idea to launch into something equally strenuous once you are out of the office. If you do, you are overloading your system. It is like driving your car with the choke out all the time. One day you will have problems with the engine. Instead, choose a sport that is fun and allows you to exercise your body in a moderate way. Look at yourself in the mirror afterwards. If you look like death warmed up, you are overdoing it.

If you are not interested in sports or if you don't like going to classes, then at least change your routine when you come home in the evening. Doing things the same old way gives you too much time to brood. Get into different clothes, sit down and talk to your partner, make love in the living room instead of the bedroom (send the kids to the cinema first!), listen to music instead of watching TV, take a bath by candlelight or take your partner out for dinner. Celebrate that you are alive, despite your work.

Make it a point to separate your private life from your work. Do not allow work to take over every aspect of your life. Your private life is just as important. People who live only for their work find it particularly hard when they retire because they have never cultivated any private interests outside work, and suddenly there is this great gap in their life. The job has gone, and nothing else is there to replace it.

I am constantly irritable, aggressive or tearful

These are the signs that occur a bit further down the stress spiral. If you are usually quite patient and cheerful, then irritability and tearfulness constitute a temporary change in your personality. You are not yourself anymore.

Irritability, aggression and tearfulness have one thing in common: they are variants of fear. Some people withdraw when they are afraid (tearfulness), others attack (irritability, aggression), but the underlying reason is the same.

The feeling of being cornered exerts such pressure on the person that they are virtually beside themselves. When they are in this state of mind they do or say things that are not at all typical of that person and, once they have simmered down again, they regret what they said, but by that time the damage is already done and often difficult to repair.

While tearfulness does not have a harmful effect on others, irritability and aggression do. They can be quite disturbing for other people around the stressed person. What usually happens is that people lower down in the pecking order are the ones that have to bear the brunt of the attacks.

Constant irritability will cause ripples further out than you might think. Being in a bad mood about something that happened at work is not something you leave behind once you shut your office door. You carry it home with you and, if you did not get a chance of letting off steam because you were in a meeting all day and your secretary disappeared off to the loo every time you came into the office, then you may start letting it out on your partner or your children. Even if you don't *yell* at them, you are still creating an atmosphere and everyone tiptoes around you – the children vanish into their rooms, your partner asks you what the matter is and you say, 'Nothing! Can't I even eat my dinner in peace?' Then your partner is upset and won't speak to you and, suddenly, it dawns on you: nobody loves you.

There is a very high divorce rate in marriages where one or both partners are in jobs where they feel constantly under pressure. The stress is passed on, in the above example, from one partner to the other, and from that partner to the children.

Stressed adults can actually cause their children to develop illnesses or problems like bed-wetting, hyperactivity, and spasms. It has been shown that children have recovered from their symptoms as soon as their mother or father underwent treatment for stress.

An imbalance in one part of the family system will always lead to other problems within that system. In a way, the problematic child serves as a scapegoat and is quite useful to the parents because now they can look on the *child* as the disturbing element in the family, rather than looking at their own problems that have led to the marital relationship not working properly. That is also why it is very difficult to get parents to consent to come into therapy. They will argue that it is their child that has the problem, not them.

If you *like* your job and don't want to leave it, it will be necessary for you to adopt a new attitude. The day has 24 hours – for everyone. If you have no time left at the end of the day to enjoy what you have achieved, then you are doing something wrong. Start creating little islands of peace for yourself.

- If possible, don't take any phone calls for the first ten minutes at work.
- Relax. Take a mental step back from your work. Check your breathing, your jaws, shoulders and hands. Make sure they are loose, rather than tensed up.
- Remind yourself of successes you have had, of times when you did well and surpassed yourself. It does not matter if it happened yesterday or 20 years ago, success is success. *Thinking* about success *creates* success.
- Ask yourself at the end of the day whether you have done your best. If you have, then there is no more you can do. If you have not been able to achieve everything you wanted to achieve, you have still done your best. Make a note of what still needs doing and leave it on your desk for the next morning. Once it is down on paper it is out of your mind.
- If you remember other things in the course of the evening, write them down at home so you won't forget.
- Start thinking whether you are leading the life you want to lead.
- Make a conscious effort to speak, walk and eat slowly. Start with one thing, whichever seems easiest. Get someone to remind you of your resolution. Do things in slow motion, deliberately. If you slow down your actions your mind calms down too.

Any sense of relaxation after a holiday is gone the moment I step into the office on the first day back

Holidays and the feeling of relaxation they create should last at least a little way into the first few days of work. If they don't, then you either did not manage to relax on holiday or you may be in the wrong job or at the wrong level.

Take the time to sit back and think about your job. Does the type of work you do appeal to you? Is it in harmony with your moral values? Does it enable you to display your talents? What is the atmosphere like – relaxed or uptight? Do you like going into work in the morning or do you dread it? Do you generally feel successful at what you are doing? Are you being paid enough? Do you have to travel a lot in your job? If you do, does this cause any problems in your private life? If you did not choose the job you are in, who chose it for you? Are you still trying to please your parents who wanted you to take over the family business? Are you a civil servant because that was considered a proper job at the time? Were you urged to start earning money when you would have preferred to go on with your education?

I am not for a moment suggesting that you should hand in your notice tomorrow and become a landscape gardener or a dog breeder in a remote part of the country. It is, however, important to be clear about the motives that underlie your choice of profession.

Should you find that you are not really doing what corresponds to your interests then you can start amending this gradually. You may find that the job as such is fine but that your strength lies in, say, the administrational side rather than in management where you are now. A vacancy may come up where the emphasis is more on administration and you may be able to change over. You will only be able to grasp the opportunity if you are aware of your preferences.

On the other hand, you may not be particularly keen on your job, but feel that there is no chance for you to leave it or change within the company at the moment. In that case you may want to counterbalance the lack of stimulation you receive at work by attending evening classes or courses that help you promote your real interests. These classes don't have to be educational, they can be totally 'useless', as long as they are fun.

One thing is important: no matter *what* job you do, do it to the best of your ability. This is crucial for your self-esteem. Even if you are scrubbing floors, you should make sure that the job is done properly. If a job is worth doing, it is worth doing well. Concentrate on what you are doing. Don't type a letter and hand it in for signature when you have not checked it for mistakes first. And don't let your boss get away with giving you vague instructions. If he or she wants good work, he or she will have to explain things properly. Take pride in your work. It is a reflection on you. If you are sloppy doing your job, what other things are you careless about?

Note: The outside reflects the inside.

I have had sexual problems since I started feeling so stressed

This is another unpleasant physical side-effect of stress: your pleasure centre closes down. In times of war, amusement arcades are the first to go.

As I explained previously the body reacts to stress by getting ready for fight or flight. The reproductive drives only stand in the way of this reaction and are therefore toned right down. The body tenses up, particularly in the back, shoulder and stomach regions and, if you are unable to relax, then that is where the tension is going to stay. To become sexually aroused, however, you have to let go of this tension, but you can only do that if you stop thinking about the problems that initiated the tension in the first place.

Here, once again, is a good example of how your thinking influences your bodily functions. There is a direct connection between the conscious and subconscious mind, between the brain and the nervous system. Sex is one of the last remaining instinctive drives we have and the harmonious unity of the body and mind is vital for it.

Sex starts in your head. You feel aroused because you think about a person you love, because you look at a stimulating picture, because you dream about something that turns you on. In other words, your mind has to be engaged in thoughts or pictures that have an arousing effect. As a consequence, your body relaxes, your muscles become floppy and the blood rushes dutifully to all the appropriate parts of your anatomy, making them feel wonderfully alive.

Sex is always accompanied by imagining situations with a sexual content: try and get aroused while thinking of yesterday's lunch. I promise you it won't work. It works even less if you think of something upsetting because thinking of a stressful situation creates physical tension that is exactly the opposite of what you need to engage in sexual activity. Sex does not happen if you are hypernervous and irritated. In this state people cannot bear to be touched, let alone be touched in a sexual way.

The fact that you have sexual problems indicates that you are either physically totally exhausted or that you cannot switch off from the things that cause you to react with stress. Your body is constantly in top gear and can no longer come down to a normal level. Once you are in this state, it is as if your nervous system becomes over-sensitive. When you are very stressed it is almost as if you become 'allergic' to problems. The slightest hint of trouble gets all stress signals blinking immediately. The same problem would not affect you at all if you were in a more relaxed state.

In this way the body-mind connection becomes a vicious circle once you start being over-stressed: problems aggravate stress, stress aggravates problems. You are less capable of solving the problem and consequently you feel less and less competent and more and more under pressure to perform well. It is the same in bed. The harder you try to achieve an erection or an orgasm, the harder you try to hold back to prevent a premature ejaculation, the less you can do it.

Note: The more will-power you employ to reach your target the less you can do it.

Sex has nothing to do with determination, it has to do with relaxation and imagination. Your body cannot get ready for sex if your mind is wandering off all the time so that you cannot concentrate on making love.

I have just had a heart attack

And it did not come out of the blue either, did it? You have had pains in your chest for a while and also on the inside of your arm. Before that you have had problems sleeping, problems relaxing, headaches, palpitations, high blood-pressure and a general feeling of being run down.

Your doctor may have told you that you were running the risk of a heart attack unless you stopped working so hard, but it was easier to take tablets to get rid of the headaches, to get the blood-pressure down and to knock you out in the evening so that you could sleep. It does not matter whether you take sleeping pills or drink half a bottle of vodka to get you ready for bed. Neither does you any good. The side-effects of sleeping tablets and alcohol are well known these days.

You have had a great number of warning signals that you have chosen to ignore, so your body went one step further and forced you to stop working so hard by blowing a fuse. Now you *have* to rest because your system has collapsed.

You had a choice. You could have prevented this from happening had you done something about it voluntarily. Now you are lying in your hospital bed, you are out of action for a while, so you may as well make use of your time by thinking about what has happened and how you can prevent it from happening again. And it will happen again if you continue living the way you have lived until now.

The fact that you have had a heart attack will help you to change because it is quite acceptable to cut down on your workload and your commitments after a severe illness. People who know about your heart attack will tend to be more considerate and keep problems away from you. Make the most of this initial period. This is the best time to bring about changes in your attitude and your life-style. Remember: unless you take action and begin to run your life along different lines, your body is going to force you to change.

What were your arguments before the heart attack? How did you justify your suicidal workload? That the company could not do without you? Well, they have to now, don't they? That you did not want to be overtaken by younger colleagues? With your self-goal you have really and truly made your worst fears come true because now the company will have to find someone to replace you, and this may well be a younger colleague.

Your motives may have been noble, but they certainly were short-sighted. Has the company chairman been in recently to thank you for your loyal support, sacrificing your health for the company? I doubt it somehow. And what good is a flattering obituary in the newspaper to you if you are looking at the daisies from underneath?

This is *your* life, and time runs through your fingers like sand. Before you know it, today becomes yesterday. Life takes place daily, so make the most of it every day. You are in a live performance, not a dress rehearsal.

Achieving happiness is important and should not be postponed until next week because next week may never come for you. Be aware that today is indeed the first day of the rest of your life. Every day is precious and this is never more obvious than during a grave illness.

Begin to think about things that used to be important to you when you were younger: your family, your friends, travelling, relaxing in the sun, enjoying a hobby. Where have all these things gone? You have given them up and replaced them with work and ambition, but this is a top-heavy arrangement where the head rules and the heart suffers. Only if you readjust the imbalance are you safe from another catastrophic illness.

When you think back to the things that upset you in your job, you can see how insignificant they suddenly become compared with seeing the light of the next day. Problems become ridiculously small when they are looked at from a hospital bed in the intensive care unit.

Get things back into proportion. Work is *not* the most important thing. Happiness and contentment also lie in many other facets of life that are not work-related. You are still alive. You have been given a second chance. Take it.

I don't have time for breaks

Then make time. Breaks are important. The harder you work the more breaks you need. Breaks are not a luxury, they are a necessity. Breaks help you to clear your head, to gather new strength, to maintain an objective outlook and to preserve your health, which means that you are working more efficiently.

It is a mistake to believe that a person who works non-stop produces better and more results. Quite the contrary is true. Workaholics do not produce more than people who take breaks, and they do not produce better quality work than everyone else – they just *look* very busy. They most certainly are not the ones who come up with the best solutions for problems because they usually cannot see the wood for the trees. And they are not having any fun doing their work either. Working does not have to be a drag. Great responsibility does not mean that you have to go around with a frown on your face.

Have you noticed that there are always two groups of people in the office? One group goes for lunch regularly, the other group (usually the smaller one) eat their sandwiches at their desk, scribbling away on a report and getting breadcrumbs all over their papers. So why is it that you belong to that second group? Maybe you think that taking a break is the same thing as being lazy, but *you* know that you are not lazy, don't you? What you probably mean is that you are afraid *others* may think you are lazy. It also indicates an acute lack of confidence on your part in the quality of the work you are producing. If you felt good about your output you could take a break without worrying about it because you would feel that you deserved it.

Anyway, how do you know others are objecting to your going out for lunch? Has your boss ever said anything to that effect? If he or she hasn't, then you can assume that he or she doesn't mind. If your boss goes out for lunch, then I suggest you interpret that positively for yourself. If your boss has the right to take a break, then you automatically have the same right.

If your boss never takes lunch breaks, however, then you would do him or her a great favour by demonstrating how to do it. Just because your boss is a workaholic does not mean you have to ruin your own health in sympathy. Be decisive about going out. Put your employment contract in your drawer and look at it before you go out. It says, 'Working hours are 9 a.m. to 5 p.m., with one hour for lunch'. There it is, in black and white. I suggest you stick to your contract.

If *you* are the boss then your contract will not say anything about lunch breaks. Instead, it says a lot about perks like a company car, profit-sharing scheme and bonuses. Bear in mind that all these goodies are of no use to you if you develop an ulcer or end up with a nervous breakdown. If the company is giving you all these perks they must want you to enjoy them, and you can only do that when you are healthy.

SCRIPT

I am a constructive person with a positive outlook on life. I love myself and my body. I take breaks regularly. I relax and allow my muscles to loosen up. I am feeling comfortable. Nothing disturbs me. I am calm and collected, my breathing is regular and even. I am deeply relaxed and a great sense of calmness pervades my body and my mind. Things that used to upset me just calm and relax me now.

Whatever I do I do efficiently and effortlessly. I know that I can cope with whatever comes my way, and this knowledge makes me strong. Whatever I attempt I achieve easily. My confidence in my abilities grows daily as I go from strength to strength. I am growing stronger every day. As soon as I leave work I switch off, and when I go to bed I can go to sleep immediately. In the morning I wake up and feel refreshed and full of energy. I look forward to every new day and feel happy and confident about my work.

SHORT FORM

- Nothing disturbs me. My self-confidence is solid as a rock.
  or
- Success is a certainty. I achieve my aims easily.
  or
- Relaxation comes easy. My body recuperates quickly and I am filled with new energy after every break.

11 | Worrying and remorse

▼ ▼ ▼ ▼

- When a problem is on my mind I cannot sleep.
- I get very worried about exams and tests.
- When I am worried about something it spoils everything else for me.
- I am worried about my children.
- If only I had married another woman I would be happier.
- I feel terrible because of a mistake I made.
- I feel guilty about an injustice I have done someone.
- If only I had had a better education I would earn more money now.

Worrying and remorse are the two greatest time-wasters in the world. They use up great amounts of energy and don't accomplish anything. They don't alter the facts, they only make you feel rotten. Both worrying and remorse are bad habits, like smoking and over-eating, and there is no need to put up with them for the rest of your life.

Worrying is feeling anxious about the future. Will I be able to cope without my boyfriend? What is going to happen if I cannot pay this bill? Is my child going to pass her exams? Will I be successful in my new job? Worrying is doubting whether there will a happy ending to a situation, whether you will be able to cope. And because you are doubting you begin to conjure up images of disaster and failure.

Do you realise what that means? It means that you are imagining a negative thing when you really want a positive thing to happen!

Note: When your will-power conflicts with your imagination, your imagination will always win out.

By worrying you are not only making yourself thoroughly unhappy, you also make a negative outcome more likely. If you worry about that speech tomorrow, you are filling your mind with negative images of stumbling as you walk up on to the platform, of forgetting your lines, of having a dry mouth or a coughing fit, of stuttering, of trembling when you adjust the overhead projector, of being unable to hold the attention of your audience.

With thoughts like these on your mind the evening before the great day, you are going to spend a restless night with interrupted sleep so that when you wake up the next morning you are exhausted. This in turn reinforces your negative thoughts. You cannot think straight so you are getting even more worried about forgetting your lines and you get butterflies in your stomach. This feeling indicates that your nervous system, once again, is carrying out the orders it is receiving from your brain: 'Danger ahead, all systems on full alert.'

If you *must* think of the next day's speech, think about it as a success. The moment you feel any negative thoughts creeping in, interrupt them. Remind yourself that you are a constructive person and therefore no longer willing to indulge in disaster-thinking. As soon as a negative thought comes up in your mind, replace it with a positive one.

See yourself walking up the stairs to the platform calmly and confidently, speaking in a clear and steady voice about your topic. See people listening with interest, nodding in agreement, smiling at you, laughing at your jokes. Imagine a great round of applause at the end of the speech that you have delivered in an expert way. See yourself stepping down, feel that sense of pride and satisfaction in yourself and your achievement, see people shaking your hand and patting you on the back afterwards.

These positive thoughts will help you focus on success. If you have prepared for your speech then there is no reason why you should doubt the successful outcome.

Spend as much time thinking about success as you can. Start the moment you know that you will have to make that speech. A positive picture will imprint itself in your subconscious mind and play back automatically when the day of the speech comes. This technique works because the subconscious mind cannot distinguish whether you have done something in reality or whether you have just imagined it. Your subconscious mind just registers whatever it is you send down for storage. So, when you fill your mind with images of calmness and success in connection with your speech, then it is as if you had actually made a successful speech already. You have coupled 'making a speech' with the feeling 'calm and collected', so this is the association that is stored away and, on the day, your subconscious mind plays off the 'tape' 'making a speech is easy and is bound to be successful' and your nervous system goes along by staying relaxed.

Positive Thinking is really what happens when you are praying. You are praying to get out of a problematic situation, you are asking for a successful outcome, at the same time *thinking* about a positive outcome, thinking about the relief you will feel when the problem is sorted out. You are praying because you believe that this is your way to receive help. You now have fulfilled all the criteria to ensure a successful outcome: you imagine success and you believe in it. A prayer does not change God, it changes the person who prays.

When you are worrying about money then you may feel that you have no influence on the situation and therefore cannot stop yourself from worrying. I still maintain that, even in a difficult financial situation, there is nothing to be gained by worrying. This is probably not the first time that you were short of money. Am I right in assuming that you are reading these lines in your flat rather than in a cardboard box under a railway bridge? In other words, you managed to get your finances sorted out before. There is no reason to assume that it will be different this time.

> **Note: Just because you cannot see a way does not mean that there is no way.**

Think back to previous dilemmas and how they were resolved. The only thing to note here is that problems are always resolved in the end.

One of my clients reported that one month she was short of the money she needed to pay a bill, and she simply did not know where to get it from. Rather than worrying about it, she decided to let the matter sort itself out, and, a few days later, she received a cheque for the amount she needed as reimbursement for a pair of shoes that were faulty.

Note: Don't believe in miracles. Rely on them.

People come up with the best ideas when they are in dire straits. Being hard up is the best incentive to create a higher income. It is amazing how people can find money for things they really want. They dream of a particular stereo system, so they keep their eyes open for opportunities to earn extra money. Opportunities always arise at the right time.

If you don't get what you want, it only means that something better is on its way. If you don't get the house you put an offer on, don't be angry. It just means that this was not the right house for you.

I went out one day to buy an oriental rug. I was looking for a second-hand one, so I went to a street market. After a while I found one I liked, but I had forgotten to bring my cheque book. I went back home to get it but, by the time I returned, the trader had sold the rug to someone else. Instead of being disappointed I decided that this was a good sign because it meant a much better rug was waiting for me. A few days later I went to another market and, sure enough, found a rug that I liked even better and that only cost me half the price of the first one.

Note: Things are meant to go right.

Expect things to go right, believe that you are a lucky person. You are not deluding yourself, you are helping yourself. You are furthering your cause and you are increasing the likelihood of getting what you want.

Remorse is similar to worrying, only that it works backwards in that you feel anxious about something that happened in the past. You feel guilty or ashamed because you have made some sort of mistake, and you dwell on it. You try to push the thoughts away, but they keep coming up, reminding you, making you feel terrible about yourself. The damage, though, is done and no matter how guilty you feel, you will not be able to undo it. You cannot turn back the clock. What happened happened, so why not use it in a constructive way?

The good thing about mistakes is that we learn from them. If we did everything right all the time we would stand still. It is only when things don't work out, when we make mistakes, that we are obliged to look for new ways.

When problems come your way, don't resist them. You are at your strongest when you stay flexible. Mishaps can occur and sweep you off your feet like a tidal wave. Whether you drown in them or not depends on how you ride the wave.

Trying to swim *against* the wave is going to cost you nerves and far more energy than you can afford, and you don't stand a chance of winning. Make sure you ride on the crest of the wave. That way you don't exert any energy and you can see where you are going.

With regard to a problem, this means you will just have to let it come up to you and look at it calmly. Problems look worse the nearer you get to them. When you are faced with a problem, look at it carefully and then begin to take it apart into all its components to decide what your angle of attack has to be. The process of analysing rather than dramatising a problem helps cut it down to size and makes the solution easier to carry out.

If your husband is made redundant, start tackling the problem immediately. Sort out your financial situation, get the family together and see how you can rearrange life to fit the new situation. Can other family members contribute to the income? Do you expect difficulties finding a similar job where you live at the moment? If so, are jobs available in other parts of the country?

Take the example of a toolmaker in northern Germany who had lost his job. He had been trying for another job for over a year and his financial resources were beginning to run low when he decided to take his family on a holiday to southern Germany, just to give everyone a break.

One morning he sat in front of his caravan, reading the local paper, when he noticed that there were quite a few vacancies for toolmakers near his holiday resort. He managed to get himself an interview for the following Monday and got the job.

Another example of turning a problem around is that of a village in France with a little school that could only be kept going if there were at least 12 pupils. The day came when the number of children dropped below that number because the older pupils had left and there were no younger children to replace them as young families tended to move away from the village into the neighbouring big city. Houses were standing empty and the school faced closure unless something happened.

Instead of giving up in the face of so much adversity, the mayor put an advertisement in some of the bigger national papers to say he was looking for families with at least six children to come and live in the village, offering them cheap accommodation and local schooling. There were so many replies that they had to draw lots to find which family was to be the lucky one! The school stayed open.

When a problem is on my mind I cannot sleep

If you worry a lot about something this tends to affect your sleep. Either you cannot go to sleep even though you feel exhausted, or you fall into a light sleep only to wake up in the middle of the night, unable to go back to sleep. A third possibility is that you sleep through the night but wake up very early, with only a couple of hours left until you have to get up.

Night-time is difficult when you have a problem. The darkness and stillness around you do not provide any distractions for your mind, and the fact that you are passively lying in bed makes it easier for your thinking to revolve around one topic because there is nothing that disrupts the process – no phone going, no doorbell, no one speaking to you and no chores to attend to. There is nothing to do. At the same time, you want to go back to sleep because you are worried that you will be very tired the next morning so, really, you are now burdened with two problems instead of one. And, as if that was not enough, you are also not thinking terribly clearly because your conscious mind is only half switched on and your subconscious mind and all its fearful feelings is interfering at the same time. The strategies to combat worrying at night are therefore different from those I recommend for day-time.

Before we look at the different sleeping problems people suffer from, let me just discuss a few general points that you should observe if you have problems with insomnia.

- Do not drink tea or coffee after 6 p.m. These drinks are stimulants, and it takes the body hours to get them out of your system.
- Drink only a little alcohol if you have to drink it at all in the evening. Alcohol is a depressant.

- Two hours before your normal bed-time you should begin to wind down, mentally as well as physically. Blood and gore on television are not the ideal images to soothe your mind, so, at least in times of great pressure, replace television with something more calming. Go for a walk or listen to quiet music, potter about in the garden or read a magazine. Prepare your body and mind gradually for sleep.
- Establish a going-to-bed routine. Go to bed at regular times.
- Do not take sleeping tablets over a long period of time.
- Do not take naps in the afternoon. Save up sleep until the evening.
- Once you have gone to bed, do one of the relaxation exercises in this book. Alternatively, you can buy relaxation tapes. Play them on your stereo or personal hi-fi as you are lying in bed.

If you cannot go to sleep when you lie in bed, make sure you have checked all the above general points. If you *still* cannot sleep, try 'paradoxical intention.' This technique has been used by many of my clients with great success. The idea behind paradoxical intention is that:

> *Note: The more will-power you employ to reach your target the less you can do it.*

This means that the harder you try to relax the less you can do it. But it also means that the harder you try to stay awake the less you can do it.

In order to make use of this law you will have to approach your insomnia from a new angle. Instead of thinking 'I *must* go to sleep', think, 'Whatever happens, I *must not* go to sleep now. I am determined to stay awake all night. I must make every effort to keep my eyes open. Under no circumstances will I close them, not even for a second. I must stay awake at any price.' Then really make an effort to stay awake. You will see that it is going to become exceedingly difficult to keep your eyes open. Persist though, really *will* your eyes to stay open. The harder you try it the less you can do it and, before you know it, you are asleep.

If you wake up in the middle of the night, don't get annoyed with yourself, just turn over on to your other side and make sure you are in a comfortable position that allows you to go back to sleep as soon as you are ready.

Imagine that you can see yourself lying in bed, as if you saw a film about yourself. Picture yourself removing all thoughts out of your head (my thoughts always look like beansprouts for some reason) and put them in a little cloth bag. Tie up the bag securely and then see yourself get up, walk out of the bedroom, into the kitchen, and there imagine how you put the bag away into one of the cupboards. Then, imagine yourself walking back to your bedroom and lying down again, just as you are lying now. Then begin to repeat in your mind one of the Short Forms on page 93. Repeat the Short Form in batches. Think the sentence 10 times without stopping, then immediately afterwards 20 times without any breaks in between, then 30 times.

Try and take in the meaning of the sentence. If you can't, don't let that put you off. The meaning will arrive in your subconscious mind anyway. And, of course, it is very boring to repeat something over and over again. It is so tedious that it sends you to sleep, and it has the added benefit that you block out any worries because you override negative thoughts with your positive ones.

Another way of dealing with waking up during the night is to get up and do something soothing. Listen to your relaxation tape again, listen to music, read the Script. Just take it as one of those things in life that happens sometimes – no need to get all het up. Of course you would be fresher in the morning if you had slept through, but being annoyed or anxious about not getting enough sleep will only make it worse.

If you cannot sleep, then at least don't be in a bad mood about it. The more you resist a situation the more difficult you make it for yourself to get to grips with it.

If you can sleep through the night, but wake up very early in the morning, you should still make the effort to go back to sleep, even if it hardly seems worth it. You have to gradually train your body to sleep longer.

Once the nervous system is upset it takes a while to settle down again, even if your bad patch is already behind you and the problem that worried you is now resolved. Your body usually lags behind and takes a while to catch up with normality, so use a Short Form in the way described above – even if it does not send you back to sleep but only calms you down.

When you do this regularly you will see that one morning your body 'forgets' to wake up early, and, once the habit has been interrupted, you will slip quite easily back into your normal sleeping pattern where you don't wake up until the alarm rings.

SCRIPT

The soft, soothing night enfolds me gently. Everything around me is quiet. Nature is at peace, drawing me gently into her welcoming arms. I am part of nature and in harmony with everything around me. My mind is soothed, my body is relaxed as I am falling gently back into tranquillity. All my day-thoughts float away like little white clouds in a summer sky, leaving my mind at peace. With every minute that ticks by, my thoughts get hazier. I am leaving the world behind. I am drifting off into pleasant dreams as my body relaxes into deep and natural sleep. With every breath I take, I drift into deeper and deeper relaxation.

SHORT FORM

- I release my day-thoughts now. The solution to my problem is already underway.
  or
- I leave the solution to my problem to my subconscious mind so that a solution can present itself to me in the morning.
  or
- I am drifting away into the night. I am one with nature. I am quiet inside.

I get very worried about exams and tests

You have every reason to be worried if you have failed to do the necessary work to pass your exam. In that case the only solution I can offer is that you sit down and revise. This is going to cut down on the time that is available for worrying and it increases your chances of passing the exam.

Go about your revision systematically. Divide up what you have to learn into manageable parts and then dedicate one day to every part. Make sure you understand what you are reading before you go on with the next part. Leave enough time in your revision schedule to go over what you have revised if you want to make sure the material is well memorised. Frequent repetition helps material to sink in better.

If you are going for a driving test, then you will not do so, I hope, unless you feel you can do all the tasks that are required. On other occasions you may have to do a test where you cannot do any preparatory work, but even for IQ tests and personality tests you will find books that provide you with tips on how best to deal with these sorts of assessments.

Whatever the test or exam you have to sit, bear in mind that the results can only be relative. They are relative to your own constitution that particular day and they are relative to whether the examiner had had another row with his wife that morning or not. There are certain areas that are more difficult to assess objectively than others. An essay about a literary topic, for example, may attract greater variance in grading than a maths test.

A well-known magazine in Germany asked a famous author to write an essay on a topic that 18-year-old students had been presented with in their exams. The magazine then handed this essay to a number of grammar school teachers who would normally mark these 18-year-olds' exam papers. The teachers were told that the essay was written by a student. The results were amazing: the author's essay received grades ranging from A to U, with some teachers calling it 'remarkable' and others marking it as 'a lot of rubbish'.

In your driving test, one examiner will pass you even if you need several attempts at getting the car to reverse around that corner, another one will fail you. When your overall performance is satisfactory, you will get away with imperfections, so your best bet is to prepare well, practise conscientiously and go into the test with the knowledge that what you can do during practice you can do in a test too.

Observe the following steps when you are getting ready for an exam or a test.

- **Prepare well**
  Be professional about the way you prepare. Put your heart into it so that you can say to yourself that you have truly done your best.

- **Take breaks during revision**

  Do not exhaust your memory by trying to cram in too much material in one go. The breaks should be regular – every hour or two – and need not be long (10 to 15 minutes is quite sufficient). Go for a walk around the block or go to another room in the house. That way you allow the material to sink in.

- **Eat properly**

  Your body needs to function well, make sure it gets what it needs. Fat light meals rather than very rich food, and try to stay away from junk food if you can. Several small portions are better than one big meal because big meals tend to make you tired. Bloodflow is diverted from the brain to the stomach area to help digestion, which is why it becomes difficult to maintain concentration or think clearly when you have had a large meal.

- **Half a day before the exam or test, stop preparing.**

  Put the books away, don't do any more driving. What you don't know by now you will never know.

- **Spend the last half day before the exam or test doing light physical exercise and relaxing.**

  Go for a swim, go to the cinema, take your mind off the exam.

- **Make an endless tape with the Script that follows.**

  Speak in a calm, clear voice and record the Script two or three times onto the tape. Listen to the tape during breaks, in the evening before you go to sleep and during the last half day before the big event. That way you ensure that the positive messages have time enough to 'grip'.

SCRIPT

I'm secure in the knowledge that I have prepared well for my exam. My thorough revision is now paying off. Everything I have revised is ready in my mind to be recalled easily and effortlessly during the exam. I am a great success. I can see myself walking into the examination room, perfectly calm and relaxed and with great confidence. I am sitting down at my desk, breathing calmly, at ease. I look at the other students. I see some people I know and I smile at them. I am calm and collected. When we are being asked to turn over the question paper, I do so and begin quietly reading through it. I understand every single question immediately and begin to tackle them one by one, calmly and efficiently. My mind is fully concentrated on what I am doing, my hand is steady, my writing easy.

Everything I have revised is now at my disposal. The answers come to me as soon as I read the questions, easily and effortlessly. I work steadily and systematically and finish my paper in good time. The invigilator comes around now to collect all the papers, and I get up and leave the room, feeling a great sense of satisfaction. I know I have done well and I feel a great sense of pride in my achievement.

SHORT FORM
- My revision is paying off. I remember easily and answer all questions correctly.

SCRIPT
(Add to this script as appropriate. If you expect other tasks as well as a three-point turn and a hill start, just add them in a similar way to the Script.)
I am well prepared. I am confident about my driving skills and I go into my driving test knowing that I will pass. I can see myself and the examiner getting into the car. My mind is clear and I feel happy and relaxed. I do all the right things quite automatically. My practising is paying off now.

I am confident and unflappable. I am tackling all the tasks competently. I can feel how everything is going very well. I can see myself doing a **three-point turn** (at this point, describe in detail how you go about doing the three-point turn and see yourself doing it). **Then I drive on, all the while calm and collected. The examiner is pleased with my performance. Now he asks me to do a hill start. I know I can do this easily and I get it right immediately** (again, describe in detail how you do the hill start – putting on the handbrake and so on – and *see* yourself doing it). **Everything is going well, and it really is ridiculously easy.**

Finally, the examiner asks me to stop and checks on my knowledge of the Highway Code. I answer every question promptly and correctly. I find it easy to recall what I revised. The examiner assures me that I have done very well and I feel happy and proud at having passed my driving test so easily.

Short Form
- I am a competent driver. I pass my test easily and effortlessly.

In this context, I would also like to add a further Script that readers who have passed their driving test, but have not driven since may find useful. Often people lose courage when they have not had any practice for a while and are reluctant to try for fear of causing an accident through their inexperience.

Script
I am a circumspect driver. I have passed my test and I have proved that I am capable of driving a car in a safe way. I look forward to going back to driving. A great sense of calmness spreads through me as I pick up the car keys and step outside. My breathing is calm, my mind is collected. I unlock the car door and get in. I am in my element. As I am sitting in the seat, all that I have ever learnt about driving comes back to me. I remember everything clearly and I am beginning to feel confident. I switch on the engine. The car starts immediately. I check the rear mirror, set the indicator and pull out into the street when it is safe. I drive along, competently steering the car. I am in full control of every situation. I know I am doing well and I feel a great sense of pleasure about my newly gained freedom. I am careful and circumspect whenever I am driving.

Short Form
- I drive confidently and carefully. I enjoy being in control.
  or
  Driving gives me pleasure. I find it easy and enjoyable.

When I am worried about something it spoils everything else for me

When you are worried about your work you cannot enjoy the party you are going to. When you are worried about finances you cannot enjoy your daughter having passed her exams. When you are worried, nothing else counts. Your worry overshadows any pleasant event that could help you keep up your morale.

Anything positive that happens is cancelled out by your worry – happiness and enjoyment are postponed until your problem is solved. This attitude can become a nuisance when you are constantly worried about something, as this is bad news for your happiness.

I have noticed that people who react like that when they are worried are also people who feel guilty and blame themselves for a lot of things. It is as if they punish themselves in some way by not allowing themselves to be happy, and the worry is really only an excuse to be able to chastise themselves. There are a variety of reasons why someone should act like that, but there is one characteristic that emerges quite clearly and that is a profound lack of self-esteem.

This usually originates in childhood where a person was continually put down, humiliated or physically abused. All this makes a child feel guilty. This may seem an odd reaction, but we must not forget that a child has no way of assessing *why* the parents treat her as they do. A child lives in a world that focuses only on her own person, so if she gets beaten or criticised it is because of something she has done. If the child has not done anything then the reason must be that she is not worthy of the parents' love. She is bad and therefore not lovable.

Another reason why people feel guilty is that there may have been an attitude in the family that it is 'wrong', or even sinful, to have fun and enjoy oneself, and that the only acceptable way of life is to consider it a vale of tears and behave in a grave manner. Happiness is therefore a frivolity that you have been made to feel guilty about, and you consequently suppress it dutifully. Some people are literally afraid of being happy because they expect something awful to happen if they are not continuously on their guard.

For any of the above reasons, some people find it difficult to permit themselves to have a good time, so whenever a problem occurs they subconsciously heave a sigh of relief because now everything fits into their mental picture of the world again.

This is not to say that they do not suffer because of their constant worrying. They wish they did not feel compelled to worry so much and, yet, something within them will not allow them to change. In these cases it is often necessary to discover the subconscious reasons why they feel guilty before any change can be brought about in their mental attitude (see pages 177–185).

You may well have recognised some of the above examples as typical for your childhood. Alternatively you may be under a great deal of stress at the moment and things are getting on top of you so that you cannot enjoy life. Whatever the reason is for one problem dominating your life, please bear in mind that good things occur even in times of trouble – we just do not take any notice of them because we are too busy worrying. It is therefore important to remember the following points.

- Things are meant to go well. Life is supposed to be enjoyable (no matter what anyone else has told you in the past).
- You *deserve* to be happy and carefree. Everyone is given this right. See to it that you make use of it.
- Focus your attention on pleasant things, no matter how small. Shift your perspective from *negative* to *positive*. The more time you give to a problem, the bigger it becomes in your mind. Fill your mind with positive things and there will be no room left for negative thoughts.
- Watch the way you speak. Make sure you talk in a moderate way, cut out dramatics. Speak calmly and reasonably about things that concern you, don't exaggerate. Keep the pitch of your voice down and choose words that tone down the problem. This will help you keep your feelings under control.

SCRIPT
I have a good life. My attention is focused on all the positive things that are happening in my life every day. The more I become aware of the good things around me, the happier I feel within myself. I deal with problems calmly and

efficiently as and when they occur. Problems are friendly and I am confident that I can always solve them competently and easily. As my confidence in myself and my abilities grows daily, my life becomes more and more enjoyable. I leave the past behind me and make a new start now. I shed sadness and anguish and step out into the world as a new, positive person. I am looking forward to my new life.

Short Form
- I look at the bright side. My positive outlook gives me strength.
  or
  I overcome any problems easily. My life is enjoyable and positive.

I am worried about my children

Parents have certain ideas about what sort of person they want their children to become. In some families this starts even before the child is born.

I have known families where there was great disappointment about the arrival of a daughter because they wanted a son ('It's *only* a daughter!'). A mother who, deep down inside, hates men, may be equally unhappy about having a son rather than a daughter. This attitude is very difficult for the child to cope with and often children try to adapt to the best of their ability to match the desired image.

When you worry about your children it means that they momentarily do not match your expectations. You may have thought of your son as a future scientist, and all he wants to do is to join the local amateur dramatic society. You may have wanted your daughter to go into an office job and now she announces that she is going to train as a carpenter. You may have wanted a child who is suave and sophisticated and what you get is a kid who cannot walk the length of a room without getting his legs in a twist and knocking something over. In other words, there is a constant conflict between what you *expect* and what you *get.*

When you made all these plans for your child's future you wanted it to be happy and to do better than you did. Children are often used to make up for what their parents missed out on. You could not go to university when you were young and so your child has to go whether he wants to or not. You want to see an old dream fulfilled, and your son has to do it for you. Tough luck that he always wanted to join the police force!

So, when you are making plans for your child's future, check carefully what your motives are. What is in it for you if your son becomes a doctor? Do you expect the neighbours to treat you with more respect? Do you think that your friends will envy you? *Why* are you so opposed to your daughter becoming a carpenter? Because the neighbours might laugh? Because your friends might pity you?

In the midst of all these thoughts, don't forget that your children have their own personality and, according to that personality, will try to find their own way through life – provided you give them the freedom to do so. If you try and press your child into a mould that does not match his or her personality, you will have permanent fights, scenes, slamming doors and a generally unpleasant time. Or you will have peace and quiet on the outside, only to find out that your child says 'yes' to you and goes and does exactly the opposite behind your back.

You may mean well, but there is no way you can save your children from getting hurt as they grow up. They have to go through their own experiences in order to learn. You can advise and support, but you should not try and run their lives for them.

In many ways, children stay the strangers they were to you when they were first born. Even if they are similar to you in aspects of their character, looks and so on, they are also different from you in other respects and therefore not predictable.

Rather than worrying about your children, you can help bring out the best in them, to discover and develop all their talents and abilities, whatever they may be.

Being a parent is a general task rather than a specific one. You can teach them patience so that they can see themselves through difficult situations later on in life. You can give them time so that they understand that someone cares about them and so that they are capable of caring for someone else later in life. You can give them love, because that is the true foundation upon which their future life is based. You can show them respect, because that is the only way they are going to learn to respect themselves and others. Treat your child as you would like your child to treat you.

All these things do not mean that you have to give in to every demand your child makes or that you have to avoid rows at all costs. But be honest with your child and take into account that children are frightened easily because they are newcomers to life and the world. Listen to them and let them have their say. If at all possible, try and find a compromise to include your child's wishes as well as your own. If you really want your child's happiness, then take it seriously and keep up communication at all times, no matter what happens. You can only help and support if you are open and willing to listen, even though your opinions may differ.

Whatever values or types of behaviour you want for your child you will have to exhibit yourself: don't expect your child to be patient if you blow your top at every opportunity, don't expect your child to love you if you cannot show your child love, don't expect your child to be courageous when you are cowardly. Children copy what they see, they are a reflection of what happens in their immediate environment, and you as parents are the closest people in your children's lives for a long time. If you are happy with yourself you can help your children become people who are content with their lives – whether they end up as professors or road-sweepers.

If you want love and not just gratitude from your children, stop worrying and start helping them to bring out the best in themselves. Acknowledge the fact that they are individuals with their own personalities and respect them as people in their own right. Don't waste any more time worrying about them. Speak to them and find out what is wrong. Listen to what they are saying without judging and try to find a solution together. Worrying about your children signals a breakdown in communication. You are the adult: do something about it.

If only I had married another woman I would be happier

(This also comes in the form of, 'My Wife Does Not Understand Me'.)
Sentences starting with 'if only' are usually uttered by people who blame their problems on someone else. As they are not prepared to take responsibility for

their *own* misery, they look elsewhere for the culprit. When things go wrong and you see such a person smile, it is probably because they have just thought of someone they can blame it on …

So if, indeed, you had married another woman you would probably *still* be sitting here telling a friend that you have made the wrong choice. What is *really* the problem? Have you stopped talking to one another? Have you given up doing things together? Has sex become boring? Do you feel that you are not getting any support from your wife when it comes to your professional career plans? All these things were OK when you first got married. You bought your first home together, the children were born, you got a better job after a while and now you suddenly realise that things have gone stale. Everything has become predictable, routine has taken over.

One of the things about living together is that you become less active. As a single person you have to develop initiative to make your own entertainment. You have to go out and make friends if you don't want to be lonely. Once you have found someone and you move in together, however, there is no need for all these activities. You have a partner, you are in love and still getting to know one another, so you have enough excitement at home. Then you struggle through financial problems together, bring up the children, build up your career or both your careers and, before you know it, you are 45. You have both become domesticated and settled into life as a couple. The comfort is there, the excitement has gone. The chores are out of the way, and now you are left with a great void.

It is not just your wife who has become boring, you yourself have lost lustre. Remember that what you see in others is usually a reflection of what you are yourself. If you make sex into a routine it is hardly surprising that you don't get an enthusiastic response. If you refuse to talk to your wife about things that matter to you, communication will eventually break down. If you don't make an effort to do new things together with her, life becomes dull.

There is no point in regretting having married your wife. At the time it was the right thing to do. You needed her and she needed you for whatever reason, so you got together. A relationship changes over the years and there are times when nostalgia sets in for that initial honeymoon phase of the relationship. This is when affairs happen.

Affairs are not always detrimental, as long as they are over in a short time and conducted discreetly. In some cases they can actually *save* the marriage because you realise what you have in your partner. However, that is only so in the minority of cases and I would not generally recommend an affair. It is a hurtful thing to do to your partner and, should you be found out, your partner's trust in you will be destroyed for a long time to come or altogether. Also, the chances of a successful relationship with someone you meet while you are still married are minimal. Even after you have been divorced there is a great strain on any follow-up relationship, simply because you have not yet finished dealing with the divorce. Work on yourself, improve yourself, learn to live by yourself and, whatever you do, don't get married again straight away.

When you are feeling regrets about the relationship you are in (whether the relationship has been a longstanding one or not) you have two options. You can either make that relationship work again or you can quit. Just sitting there, wishing you had decided differently 20 years ago does not solve the problem.

Make up your mind what it is you want and then go for it 100 per cent. Begin to work on yourself again. Start getting involved in new things, take up new hobbies and you will become more alive again.

If you want to make a fresh start with your wife, start talking to her again. Tell her that you feel you two got into a bit of a rut and that you want to change this. Take an interest in what *she* is doing, which means putting your newspaper down when she is talking to you. Give out information about yourself and your work.

If, however, you are hoping that your wife will go off with someone else so that you have a reason to split up with her, then the truth of the matter is that you don't want the relationship to go on. In this case, too, you will eventually have to speak to your wife about it. So, don't bemoan the fact that you are stuck in a marriage that you don't want any longer – do something about it. You don't have peace of mind at the moment, and you certainly won't have an easy time until you have moved out or the divorce is through.

Breaking up is one of the hardest things to do if you have ever cared for a person. So, if you think it is the only way to deal with your present relationship, get it underway as soon as possible. There is no point in prolonging the agony.

I feel terrible because of a mistake I made

Mistakes are nothing to be ashamed of. They happen to all of us quite regularly. Mistakes are necessary to ensure that we do not stand still. They help us progress, gain new skills and further our knowledge.

Mistakes are a vital ingredient in the process of living, so if you make mistakes it means that you are active, that you are alive. Accept mistakes as part of the continuing learning process that is part of becoming the best possible person you can be.

Use mistakes to your advantage. If you have made an error, think about it carefully and analyse what went wrong. Why did the mistake occur? Did you act without thinking? Did you dither too long and consequently lost what you were after? Were you very nervous at the time and therefore made a blunder?

Once you have found the underlying reason it is much easier to avoid the mistake in future when a similar situation occurs. It is to your advantage to look closely at what went wrong. Once you have thoroughly analysed the mistake, file it away under 'Experience' in your mind. Mistakes are there to help, not to punish.

Not all mistakes are irreversible. If you buy a pair of shoes and, on getting home, realise that they don't go with the colour of your dress, you can take them back and exchange them. From this you will have learnt that next time it will save you hassle if you take the dress with you when you are trying to find shoes to go with it.

If you have shown yourself up in the past you may have done so through no fault of your own. You may have asked a friend of a friend about her husband, only to find that he left her a couple of weeks ago. You may have accused your child of something you later find out he did not do. Show greatness – apologise.

Most of the time our mistakes are not as bad as we think. You forget to pass on a message to someone from a friend and later find out that they met by chance so that the message got delivered anyway. You forget to ring up somebody about a business deal and later find out that the whole thing has fallen through already. We are often embarrassed about little things that are of no importance to others. So what if you had an accident and the ambulance men discovered that your knickers didn't match your bra? Is this really worth getting upset about? Surely not.

There is no way you can avoid making mistakes altogether. By trying to be perfect you are carrying a burden that can break your back. Go easy on yourself, forgive yourself. Repeated self-accusation leads to depression, and that is of no use at all because it prevents you from trying again and doing better the next time around. If you want to do yourself a favour, ease up on yourself.

If you were humiliated every time you made a mistake when you were little, don't carry on this dubious tradition. Just because this happened in the past does not mean it has to happen in the future, too. You have the choice now whether you want to continue along the old lines or change the rules. Why do you find it so difficult to forgive yourself? Was it a cardinal sin to make mistakes when you were a child? Were you blamed for not trying hard enough when you did something wrong? Or were you blamed for doing something on purpose when you were only clumsy? If that was the attitude you encountered at home you may now be burdened with an over-active conscience that automatically makes you feel guilty whenever you make a mistake. It is a tough job to reduce that conscience to a normal size, but it can be done. What you need is a lot of persistence. Every single time you catch yourself brooding over a mistake you made, think the situation through like a report.

Let us assume that you are a secretary and have forgotten to cancel an appointment. All of a sudden, three visitors turn up and want to see your boss who is just about to leave the office to go to a meeting. Your boss has to explain the situation, the visitors are a bit annoyed, but leave in the end and your boss is not impressed by your performance to say the least. You apologise.

A week later the episode is still on your mind. Every once in a while you feel this highly unpleasant sensation in the pit of your stomach and feel hot flushes rising to your cheeks, and there you see the scene again: the three visitors in your office, your boss explaining and you, greatly embarrassed.

It is practically impossible to prevent these thoughts and feelings from cropping up, so don't resist them. Allow them into your mind. Write yourself a note which says something like:

Last Monday I forgot to cancel an appointment. I am now taking steps to prevent this mistake from occurring again. I am now noting down the things I have to do during the day and I check my notes regularly. I am improving every day.

Every time you catch yourself feeling guilty or embarrassed about the incident again, look at the note. Occupy your mind with the *solution, not* with the mistake. If you deal with past mistakes in this manner you will notice that unpleasant feelings of guilt and remorse fade more quickly and you have spare capacity to go on to more positive things.

I feel guilty about an injustice I have done someone

It can happen that you are unfair towards someone just because you are under pressure or in a bad mood and that person had to bear the brunt of it. In a row, it can also happen that you are so hurt by something your partner says to you that you lash out verbally and go for the other person's weak point intentionally.

These outbursts can do damage to a relationship. It is therefore essential that you go and apologise for what you have said. There is no need to humble yourself or crawl, but there is definitely a need to talk it out, if only to explain why you exploded so suddenly.

Do not expect to be forgiven immediately just because you have apologised. It takes some time for the wound to heal, and the relationship needs a little while to get back to normal. The more frequently these outbursts occur, the longer it will take your partner to get over them. If you have mood swings and keep dishing out hurtful, negative statements to those around you, you are jeopardising your relationships, especially if you get insulting in the process.

There is nothing wrong with having a row as long as you do not humiliate, ridicule or accuse. The simplest way to avoid this is to make sure you start your sentences with 'I' instead of 'you'. Say, '*I* felt really angry when you kept me waiting for an hour this morning', instead of '*You* are totally unreliable!'. Say, '*I* find it very hard to cope with your temper', rather than, '*You* are an impossible bully. Everybody hates you.' By expressing your feelings in this way, you give feedback on what is happening inside you when your partner behaves in a certain manner. Say, '*I* am not at all happy with the merchandise you sent us' to the sales department, not, 'Your merchandise is rubbish'.

Present criticism or a complaint in an acceptable form. If you corner your partner by the way you are expressing yourself, the result will be unsatisfactory. Insults and aggression breed hurt and retaliation. If you expect respect and understanding you have to *give* it first.

All this does not mean that you are in this world to be what others want you to be. You have the right to be as you are at this very moment. My point is that if you experience difficulties with other people, then take any feelings of guilt as signals that you need to examine your own attitude. Guilt has served its purpose and can be dismissed once you have started thinking about yourself. Guilt should be the first step in your personal development, that is all. It should not be your constant companion. In the end you will be judged by what you have *achieved*, not by how guilty you have felt about your shortcomings.

It is your decision how you handle your feelings of guilt, whether you allow them to drag you down or whether you use them to find new ways. Guilt and remorse are useless burdens. Far too many people carry them around with them in the belief that it is their lot in life to suffer. This only demonstrates that they believe in misery rather than happiness, in bad rather than good.

Note: Things are meant to go right.

If you have done someone an injustice, be honest enough to admit it to that person. Try to rectify the situation if that is at all possible. If you cannot make up for it to that particular person, you can always help someone else instead. This is not penitence but active self-improvement. There is no need for self-contempt, shame or depression. Learn from your past mistakes and turn over a new leaf.

Don't give up if you don't succeed immediately. It took you many years to become what you are today. Any changes you desire will require time too. As long as you want to change you will also be able to see the changes through to a successful end. You will like yourself even better for having achieved your goal. You are worth it, so make the effort!

If only my parents had given me a better education I would be earning more money now

And then you would be happier than you are now, right?

What you are saying is that your happiness is dependent on a certain amount of money, and that is unobtainable because you did not get the right educational back-up when you were young. So your unhappiness today is caused by a mistake your parents made in the past.

Under the present circumstances you cannot be happy. You are imposing certain conditions on life and, unless they are fulfilled, you don't want to know. You sit in your corner and sulk. Life does not work like this, however, it works the other way round. When you are happy you will earn more money. Happiness and Positive Thinking have to happen first, and they will automatically be followed by health, wealth and good relationships with other people.

When you are happy you are relaxed. You are inspired because you have the time to listen to your inner voice. All your good qualities can come to the surface and help you achieve your aims. Reach out with confidence for whatever it is you want, be it a better education or more money. It is never too late – age is unimportant. If you have been given a wish you have also been given a way of fulfilling it.

Financial worries are something we can all do without, and it is certainly legitimate to want to be wealthy. I personally do not see any virtue in being poor. If you are poor you have nothing to give. The only people who disdain money are the ones who have not got any – and for a good reason. You only attract what you love. If you disapprove of money, then your attitude will make you miss opportunities to make money. If you think 'poverty', you will be poor. Your financial status, to a certain degree, is subject to the way you think, just like your relationships, your health and your personal and professional success.

If you have money you can set a positive example. Not only that: you can actually use that money to help others. I find this a lot more useful than declaring your solidarity with the poor.

Things are meant to work out in life, and that also goes for your finances. If you want to enjoy life you have to be financially secure. Good work should be rewarded by good pay. So, if you cannot get the money you want in the job you are in, and you really think this is due to a lack of educational back up, then you will have to do something about it. You are, after all, much more likely to succeed in further education now than when you were younger – *now* you are motivated, *now* you have the necessary maturity to see it through. If you want to get additional qualifications, you will get them. The only person who can stop you achieving that diploma or degree is, as usual, yourself.

Making money is not necessarily linked to relevant qualifications, though. The world is full of highly qualified people who don't do their jobs well. You have to love what you are doing in order to do it well. If a mother does not like being a mother, she will not make her children happy. If an accountant does not like figures, he will never get to the top of his profession. In order to be successful you have to be in harmony with what you are doing, you have to be able to immerse yourself fully in your job. People who are happy in their jobs feel more in control of their lives and are less prone to develop stress-related problems.

It is also important to know yourself well if you want to make money. You have to be aware where your strengths lie so that you can go into a field where you are able to make full use of them. A person who is good at selling will be able to sell anything – from double glazing to Christmas cards. A person who likes to take risks will do well as a racing driver, a stunt man or even a debt collector for the tax office.

Your choice of job says a lot about you as a person. Look at the job you are in now. If you have chosen it yourself, it will reflect what you think your strength is. If you are in a job that is beneath your capabilities then that reflects your lack of self-confidence: you did not feel you could go for a better job because you were not sure whether you could do it. In many an office there are employees who look at their bosses and think, 'I could do his or her job', but they never apply when the opportunity arises. This is partly due to self-doubt, partly to the fear of being disappointed: 'What if I apply and I don't get the job? Won't I feel humiliated at not having made it?', or, 'Will Personnel think it ridiculous that I am going for this job?' You may feel disappointed at not getting the job, but at least you have tried. If you think you can do more than you are doing in your present position, you *owe* it to yourself to make the effort to move up the ladder. By applying for a better job you demonstrate that you have confidence in your own abilities. You have made an important point that will be noticed by others. It is really up to you to publicise how good you are. Modesty will just hold back your career. Make sure your boss knows about your achievements, make sure he or she knows you are aiming high, and that includes you going for promotion. And if you don't get that job in the other department, just think that it is their loss, not yours. They are losing out on a capable and committed colleague and boss. Another opportunity is bound to come up soon, if not there then in another company. All you have to do is persist, and then you cannot fail.

Once you have made up your mind to go for a better job, you are already halfway there. It is only a matter of time until the appropriate vacancy turns up.

SCRIPT
I am going for the top. I am confident and I cope easily with my work. I am ready to develop further and to tackle new areas. Nothing can stop me. I look at myself positively. I am aware of my wish to progress and I am therefore wide awake to new opportunities that present themselves. I trust myself and my abilities. A higher position presents an enjoyable challenge to me. I reach out for the top with confidence. The fact that I am looking for a better job has already set the wheel of fortune in motion. The right job is on its way.

SHORT FORM
• I am going for the top. The right job for me is already in the pipeline.

12 | Loneliness

▼ ▼ ▼ ▼

- I find it hard to make new friends.
- I find it hard to speak about my feelings.
- There never seems to be anyone there when I need someone.
- If someone says 'hello' I'm stuck for an answer.
- I have lost contact with friends I used to have.
- I feel miserable on my own.
- I think that others dislike me.
- My partner has recently left me.
- I am an outgoing person, but I'm still lonely.

So *why* are you lonely? Loneliness is self-inflicted suffering. You are lonely because you *choose* to be lonely. Even if you live in a village with only two inhabitants and one dog, you still have two people to talk to. If you live in a big city there are even more people you can establish contact with – people living above you in the house, next door, across the road, people who are looking forward to talking to someone. You are surrounded by people who you can communicate with, go out with, have a good time with. There are thousands of people out there who are waiting for you to get in touch with them, to come over for a chat. Once again, it is all up to you.

You will have to go out and show your face, you will have to be *available* for communication, friendship or love. You have to welcome people into your life. If you stay away from the world and lock yourself in with your TV and a family-size bag of crisps, it is not surprising that you are lonely. People have forgotten you exist.

People may not want to contact you because you have become boring to be with. If your interests in life are limited to the next sequel of the latest soap opera, then your value as a partner for a conversation is rapidly approaching zero. You have nothing to say because you are not getting involved in life. Remember:

Note: *A person who is interested is interesting.*

A person who sits in front of their TV all the time is, like the TV programme, dull. And don't tell me you have tried to change when all you have done is walk out the front door, only to turn back when you thought the postman scowled at you. That does not qualify for a serious attempt.

Let's go through the above statements one by one.

I find it hard to make new friends

Let's qualify this statement. Is this because you are very shy or is it because you don't meet new people that it is difficult for you to make new friends? Depending on which one of the two answers applies to you, you will have to work on either your self-confidence or your social calendar.

If you are shy, has there ever been a time when you were more self-confident? What happened in your life to make you lose it? Sit down and think about it. Can you remember what you were like when you were more outgoing, more sure of yourself? If you have ever *had* self-confidence (even if this goes back many years), then it is still in you and can be revived. Try this.

- Relax.
- In your mind, go back to the time when you were self-confident. Recall the things you could do then, recall past successes in your imagination. These successes do not necessarily have to be related to a relationship, they can also concern other matters, as long as you acted in a confident way and achieved what you wanted to achieve.

Fill your mind with images of past success, but not in a nostalgic way. Use past successes as confidence boosters, use them to prove to yourself that, at the bottom of your heart, you *are* a successful and, therefore, confident person.

Note: What you can do once you can do again.

Imagine confidence and you will *have* confidence. Other people will notice it and respond in a more positive way to you. As we all know, everybody loves a winner, and if you *think* like a confident person, you *act* like one and people will *treat* you as one, so your way of thinking will ultimately make your remembered confidence become reality in the here and now.

Have you *never* felt self-confident? If you are quite sure that there is absolutely nothing positive you have ever achieved, nothing that has *ever* given you a sense of confidence, then you may have had a difficult start in life. Maybe your parents were impatient and answered for you every time somebody asked you a question. In this case, put the past behind you, because that is where it belongs. It is a waste of time to dwell on it. Realise that *you* are in control now. You *can* change your life, you *can* get rid of your old behaviour patterns. All you have to do is to decide that you are going to make a fresh start, and that is already half the battle.

If you have never had a success in your life, you will just have to invent one. Take a situation where you feel you could have done better if you had had more self-confidence and re-live it in a positive way. Try this.

- Relax.
- Close your eyes and re-make that old film, but this time with you as the hero. Picture yourself as the happy and confident winner, the person who is in control when everything around them disintegrates into chaos, the person who copes with whatever happens, the person who likes others and is liked by others.

To help yourself, observe people that find it easy to do the things that cause you problems. See how *they* act, speak, move. Think about it and adapt it so that it is acceptable to you and then imagine yourself tackling that difficult situation with ease. See yourself as a popular colleague, an interesting person, a good friend.

There is nothing wrong with being either successful or confident. It is not the same thing as being arrogant, overbearing or aggressive. Being confident means knowing what it is you want from life and liking yourself enough to make the effort to go and get it. Being confident means having achieved what you wanted to achieve in a way that is positive for yourself and others.

Carry your Script with you, read it regularly, as often as you can, until you know it by heart. Start with easy tasks. Look at other people, look them in the eyes and smile at them (only if you like them). You will be surprised how many smiles you get back. If someone does not return your smile, don't worry about it. You have just come across someone who is as shy as you used to be.

If you have a lean or non-existent social calendar, are you too busy working to have any time for social events? If you have been neglecting your private life in favour of work, make an appointment with yourself for next week. Get your secretary to mark in the diary that next Wednesday from 6 p.m. onwards you have an important meeting with MS (myself) and make sure you keep it. If *you* are the secretary and your private life is suffering because of work overload, do the same. Announce clearly that you need to leave on time because you have a crucial meeting with an important person (yourself, of course).

Get yourself and your boss used to the fact that you have a private life. Go home at reasonable times – you deserve it. You need to counterbalance work with play and there is certainly more to life than nine to five. It is also beneficial in the long-term to develop your private life. It has been shown that people who have interests outside work cope a lot better with retirement than those who have dedicated their whole lives to their work.

Ring up old friends, nice neighbours or relatives you particularly like and invite them over. Get old friendships going again because they invariably lead to new acquaintances, some of which may become new friends.

If you are a housewife with children, make sure you get out of the house every once in a while. Arrange for a friend or a babysitter to look after the children and go out. Do that course you always wanted to do. Do it while you still have the energy to do it. Once you have fallen prey to the 'housewife syndrome' it gets more and more difficult to get out of your lethargic state and to initiate activities.

By going out you will get a break from the children and the children will get a break from you. It is perfectly normal to be fed up with the little darlings – it does not mean that you are a bad mother, it just means that you need a break. Make sure you get it.

The happier you are, the happier you will make your children (and your husband). And don't be too disappointed when you find that your children are delighted at the prospect of your absence – it merely indicates that the babysitter lets them watch telly *before* they have to do their homework.

Script

I take my life and happiness in my own hands. I know that I can leave my past behind me and I have decided to make a fresh start. I am now opening up to the outside world. Slowly and gently, I am allowing others to come closer to me and I am helping them by meeting them halfway. I like other people and others like me. I am a valuable person and I take pride in myself and my achievements. From now on I take full responsibility for my happiness. Nothing can stop me now. Whatever I send out will come back to me in abundance. I send out friendship and love.

Short Form

- I like myself and others. I find it easy to make new friends.
  or
  I am a happy person. Other people like being with me. I have a lot to give.

I find it hard to speak about my feelings

You may be a good friend or partner and you may be good at listening to other people pouring their hearts out to you or speaking about their feelings, but if you want a relationship to progress beyond a superficial level, it is not enough just to listen.

Speaking about your feelings is like revealing a bit of your inner, intimate self. During the first stage of a friendship, people tend to be cautious about giving away too much about themselves. They will reveal minor feelings to 'test the water'. If the other person then reveals something about their feelings, they are prepared to go on to the next stage where they will give away a bit more.

This next stage is, however, dependent on the other person having reciprocated the confidence. If this does not happen, the relationship comes to a halt because of a lack of mutual trust. Friends become friends when there is a good balance between speaking and listening, giving and taking, trusting and being trusted.

If one of the two is not prepared to speak about their own feelings, the other person will begin to feel exposed. If you cannot admit to your own feelings within that relationship you make the other person feel insecure.

If someone tells you they like you and you like them but you cannot express your feelings, that person will feel rejected after a while. You may think that it should be obvious to them that you like them, but there really is no substitute for saying it out loud.

Note: Other people cannot read your mind.

If the *other* person has mustered the courage to speak out, then *you* need to do the same. If you can't or won't you are in danger of losing that person.

There never seems to be anyone there when I need someone

This statement may, to some extent, overlap with the previous point. If you cannot admit that you feel miserable and lonely, then others will think that you are OK. Other people cannot be expected to read your mind. If you want help then you will have to admit that you need help. There are no medals to be won for playing the hero when inside you feel like crying.

Many people are afraid of talking about their problems because they think they will make a fool of themselves if they burst into tears in the process. In severe cases where, for example, people have lost a beloved person, they are afraid that, once they start crying about their loss, they will not be able to stop crying, that once they allow their grief to come to the surface it will be so overpowering that they will not be able to overcome it. This is such a frightening prospect that they suppress their emotions, often for a long time, and that can lead to a great number of physical and psychological problems. In such cases it is advisable to seek professional help. If you cannot cry any more, even though you are going through horrific experiences and feel under great emotional pressure, look for a good counsellor who will help you sort out your problems.

If you do express to others that you need help and you do not get any, then you may want to take a closer look at your friends. Are they really friends or are they only around when they want something from you, disappearing back into the woodwork as soon as you ask *them* for a favour?

Think about it. What is it you think other people expect of *you*? Make a list of points. Now, make another list where you specify what you expect of your friends. If that second list is shorter than the first, then something is wrong. If you feel you have only duties, but no rights, if you feel that you must oblige but must not make any demands on others, then your self-confidence is somewhere below zero and in urgent need of attention.

If someone says 'Hello' I'm stuck for an answer

Well, one answer that springs to mind is to say 'hello' back, and smile.

There is nothing amazingly complicated about getting a conversation going. There is no need to display vast amounts of knowledge, wit or intelligence. Don't worry if you didn't do well at school – that has nothing to do with anything. I have had the most boring time of my life with someone who has two degrees. Always bear in mind that the great are only great because we are on our knees. This goes for your doctor, the teacher of your kids and your father-in-law, who did marginally better than you at school. And if your educational standard really bothers you, then do something about it. There are lots of evening classes that will allow you to catch up with what you missed out on when you were at school.

Observe other people. How do they go about starting conversations? You will notice that their approach varies depending on who they are talking to and in what environment the conversation takes place. There is a world of difference between the ways two people speak to each other in private or at a party. There may be differences in the ways people speak to their boss and the way they speak to a shop assistant. Some people find it easier to speak to the bailiff who has just come to confiscate their belongings than to speak to their parents. Some men are stuck for words when they are interested in a woman; some women feel the same way when they are trying to talk to a man they like. Where do your particular difficulties lie in conversation? Which is the group of people that makes you feel shy and insecure?

Just say something – you have nothing to lose. If the other person is rude to you then this is good because it means that you don't have to waste any more time on someone who obviously does not deserve it. Congratulate yourself on your common sense and lucid insight into others! If, on the other hand, the person is nice to you, then you have achieved your aim: you are having a pleasant conversation with someone. Congratulate the other person on demonstrating the good taste of wanting to talk to someone as interesting as yourself!

The trick is probably not to expect too much. You may have been sitting behind your desk for weeks, drooling every time this gorgeous member of the opposite sex went by, but don't forget that the object of your affections may not necessarily feel the same way about you. To find out, you will have to talk to him or her more than once. If you find out that she has a steady boyfriend or that he is married, don't let that get you down.

If you feel disappointed, then this is because you made assumptions beforehand. You had unjustified illusions and you have been disillusioned, but you have also shown that you are a person of action, that you can rise to meet a challenge when you think it is worth it.

It is good practice to talk to others, to make the effort to cultivate conversation, because one day you will find that other person who is *not* married and does *not* have a boyfriend, and you want to be ready for that.

Note: You have to play the pools to win.

SCRIPT
I am a friendly person. I am interested in others and I find it easier and easier to speak to other people. I am calm and collected. I speak easily and fluently. Conversation comes naturally to me. I express myself clearly. I converse in a natural manner. My self-confidence grows daily. Other people like talking to me.

SHORT FORM
- I am calm and relaxed. I speak with confidence and converse in a natural manner.

I have lost contact with friends I used to have

This can happen for several reasons. Classic examples are the 'Newly In Loves' and the 'First-Time Parents'.

'Newly In Loves' have a drastically reduced attention span when it comes to their environment and old friends. Nothing and nobody matters any more except the new partner, and they spend all their available free time together so that there is no time left to spend with friends. Whereas they might have been seeing their friends nearly every weekend, now they don't see them at all.

'First-Time Parents' are very busy with the new baby. They have to adapt to their brand new role as parents, which requires a lot of getting used to because, no matter how many books you have read on the subject, the reality *still* takes you by surprise. It is like suddenly having a total stranger in the house who makes a lot of noise and is complaining all the time in a foreign language that you do not understand. Again, there is hardly any time left to dedicate to friends.

After a couple of years, however, the novelty of the new partner has worn off and the baby can complain in no uncertain terms in your own language – and you have lost touch with your old friends.

At this point it is up to you to make a move. There is not much point sitting by the phone and waiting for someone to ring *you*. As far as your friends are concerned you have disappeared from the face of the earth. They got used to the idea that you are no longer available for parties or get-togethers and, unless you let them know that things have changed, they won't know any better.

Another reason why people lose touch with friends is that the friends have got married and they are still single. In this case it is really a matter of pot luck: if your married friend can be gently persuaded to join you for an occasional outing or to have you over, that's fine. You should certainly try a few times to suggest getting together before giving up. If you don't succeed, you may be better off concentrating your efforts on making new friends.

If, however, you feel uncomfortable as a single person in the company of couples, then the problem lies with you. If you are going to a sit-down dinner then the host usually arranges for another single person to sit next to you. If it is an informal occasion, then you don't have to worry either, because, as long as you are not too shy, you will find someone to talk to. Just get your host to introduce you to someone you would like to speak to. Or take the dish with the peanuts and approach the person you are interested in. Offer them the peanuts and use this as a conversation opener. Also, in a crowd of people it is not at all obvious who is with whom. As far as others are concerned you might have come with someone who is chatting to another group of people at the other end of the room.

I feel miserable on my own

Why? Probably because you think that you *ought* to feel miserable. Believe me, there is no such law. Being alone is not the same thing as being lonely. Having a partner is not the same thing as being happy. You can feel very lonely with a wife and three kids.

The reason why many people think that they cannot possibly be happy and content on their own is that they rely on other people for entertainment. And here again we come to the issue of responsibility. It is up to you whether you are happy or unhappy. It is up to you to provide your own entertainment, money, self-esteem and fulfilment. Create your future actively, don't wait to see what it may bring. Make sure you get what you love or you will have to love what you get. When you begin to take your life into your own hands, you will be so busy getting things sorted out that you won't have time to feel lonely. When you begin to improve your education, your social life, your job situation, you will be speaking to so many new people, making so many new friends, that you will wonder how you could ever find the time to wash your socks on a Saturday night.

Don't waste time thinking about things you want to get rid of. Thinking about problems means making them bigger, and that won't help you get rid of them.

Note: Whatever you spend a lot of time thinking about will become bigger.

Inform your subconscious mind about what you want. See yourself having achieved your heart's desire. Get into the swing of Positive Thinking. If you are positive you are attractive. If you are attractive you are successful. If you are successful you have money, friends, health and a great partner.

Learn to enjoy your own company.

- Look in the mirror and admire your face, body, hair.
- Prepare an exquisite meal, present it nicely and sit down to soft music and candlelight. Congratulate yourself on the superb company you are in.
- Treat yourself to a weekend away. Go for long walks, get away from the everyday world. Begin to think about all the things you want for the future. Make plans, think big. Only the best is good enough for a person as beautiful, intelligent, gifted and charming as yourself. Appreciate all the good things about yourself. I promise you this makes a pleasant change from thinking about all your faults and shortcomings.
- Put your favourite CD on as loud as you dare and pretend you are the singer.

I think that others dislike me

Do you think that a lot of people dislike you or is it just one particular person? If it is just one particular person, then you probably already have an idea as to why you two have a problem. If you don't know why you do not get on, I would strongly recommend that you ask him or her.

If you have problems with lots of people, then start by checking if you are doing any of the following things.

- Are you pessimistic about everyone and everything?
- Are you talking ill about others behind their back (see The Backstabber page 42)?
- Are you very shy and dither a lot (see The Mouse, page 38)?

- Are you prone to the ALG syndrome (Acting Like God, see The Patroniser, page 36)?
- Do you have bad breath or body odour?
- Do you interrupt others all the time when they speak?
- Do you have to be the centre of attention no matter what?
- Do you ridicule others?

If any of the above points apply, you may notice that everyone disappears or stops talking as you enter the room. It can sometimes be difficult to assess whether you are doing any of these things because they have become a habit and you don't notice them any more. Ideally there is a person you know whose judgement you trust, someone who likes you and who will give you a kind but honest opinion about yourself.

Have you had any criticism lately concerning your behaviour? Take it seriously. Was the criticism justified? If you don't understand what the other person is complaining about, say so. Don't accept criticism that you don't even understand and then toss and turn in bed at night. Ask! Once you know what it is others object to in you *and* if you consider it a justified complaint, make a point of working on that weak point.

If you feel that the complaints about you are unfair or exaggerated or that they seriously affect your well-being and health in any way, you may have to walk out of that situation, be it a relationship or a job, *but not before you have tried to talk about it with the person or people concerned.*

If you just have a very general feeling that others don't like you, then it is far more likely that it is the other way round: it is you who does not like other people. Maybe you are afraid of others, afraid of getting hurt.

Did you get hurt badly when you were little? Do you find it difficult to trust others? Are you suspicious that others are trying to pull the wool over your eyes or get the better of you? When someone laughs behind you on the bus, do you automatically assume that they are laughing about you? If you are answering 'yes' to these questions, then it means that you don't like yourself. If you don't like yourself you won't be able to like others, and this will show.

Note: Whatever you send out to others will come back like a boomerang.

Start working on your self-confidence. If your past dominates you and you cannot get to grips with your problems by yourself, get someone else to help you (see pages 177–185), but before you do try using the Script at the end of this chapter for the next three weeks. Many people find that this is sufficient for them to make positive changes in their life.

There is no need to put up with a lack of self-confidence.

My partner has recently left me

And now you sit at the bottom of a deep black hole and cannot get out again. Splitting up is bad enough, but being left is a lot worse because it seems to suggest that you are not pretty, handsome, intelligent, amusing, sexy, interesting, lovable enough to be with. Next to losing your job it is probably the ultimate blow to the ego.

You are feeling terrible, you have tears in your eyes all the time, you feel desperate, thinking, 'I'll never find anyone else again!' and angry, thinking, 'That bastard/bitch! And to think that I gave him/her that expensive watch for Christmas!', with a fair bit of self-pity thrown in for good measure.

There is nothing wrong with these feelings. Get them out of your system. Listen to a really soppy song and have a good cry. It is a great relief to cry. If you feel angry, punch a cushion for half an hour. When you start feeling angry at your ex, you are halfway out of that hole again. Anger puts you back into an active mode; all you have to do is channel that energy in a constructive way.

You may find that there are already others willing to fill the vacancy as your live-in-lover. This is of course very convenient and tends to speed up the recovery process no end. It does not mean, however, that you are really over it. It is a bit like giving up smoking: you know the damn things are no good for you, but you still want them. You have not really finished with them until you can look at one and not feel the slightest stir of emotion. In the same way, whoever steps into the shoes of your ex-lover stands little chance with you because you are really just using them as a comforter and stop-gap. Be aware of that. Relationships on the rebound rarely work out.

So, if you don't have a willing replacement at hand, you should use this invaluable opportunity to channel all the energy that has suddenly been set free to work on your career and develop yourself in other areas of life. Do it before you get into another serious relationship, before that pleasant but counter-productive inertia sets in again. It is *between* relationships that you have the greatest chances to start new things, move into new fields and build yourself up to become a stronger and more confident person.

You cannot count on someone else being around all the time, carrying you. Relationships are not automatically forever. They require a sense of commitment and flexibility on both parts. You can have differences of opinion, fights a partner can be seriously or permanently injured, be made redundant, die suddenly. We all hope these things will never happen, but they do. It is during these difficult times that you will need something to fall back on, and that something can only lie within yourself. If you have not acquired a sense of self, a trust in your own abilities and a generally positive outlook on life, a disaster will hit you doubly hard.

Once you have cried enough about your ex-partner, get out of that hole and look around you to see how you can start doing something about your life that helps you progress. Concentrate on yourself for a while. Your age is immaterial in all this. There is always room for improvement, whether you are 18 or 75. There is always another partnership on the horizon, no matter how many wrinkles you have. Do not worry about age. My personal motto is that if a man complains about my wrinkles, the *man* has to go, not the *wrinkles*.

You are as young as your hopes and as old as your fears. As long as you have ambitions, as long as you make plans, you are young. When you have given up hope you are old. Hopelessness is a result of not understanding the basic principles of living. There is *always* a way. Just because our minds are too limited to see it does not mean the way does not exist. Once you can believe this fundamental truth you won't have to worry ever again.

SCRIPT

- **I am using my free time to my best advantage. I am creative and productive. Now is my time to develop further, now is my chance to take a** big step forward. All my energies are engaged in helping myself progress. I am directing all my efforts to positive new aims. I believe in myself. My inner strength carries me through.

SHORT FORM
- This is my big opportunity. I am constructive and positive and I begin to work on my future.

I am an outgoing person, but I am still lonely

You may be the type of person who is very popular, has lots of friends, but still feels that he or she just cannot find a partner. Everyone tends to come to you with their problems to receive advice and help and encouragement. People ring you up at all hours to tell you about the latest turn in their disastrous relationship and keep you on the phone for hours. You are everybody's best friend but nobody's lover.

Compared with everyone else's problems you find your own fairly insignificant, so you continue to take desperate phonecalls in the middle of the night and arrive at the office the next morning, bleary-eyed and exhausted from lack of sleep. Please become aware that you are *not* everyone's emotional rubbish dump.

It is important to stand by your friends during times of trouble – that is fine – but beware of the whiners. These are people who are not really interested in doing anything about their problem, they just enjoy moaning (see The Martyr, page 39). If you listen long enough to people like that, you will become depressed too. If you allow yourself to become engulfed by other people's problems you can easily 'catch' their anxiety and hopelessness. You have the duty to protect yourself against this happening to you, so sort out the whiners who are just using you from friends who genuinely need and want help.

Give people your time to start off with, speak to them, suggest ways of dealing with their problem, then see if they actually do anything to resolve their difficulties. If they don't, then you are obviously unable to help them any further.

If somebody is just using you for their purposes, you need to tell them that, from now on, you are only prepared to talk to them if they have something positive to say. Don't be afraid that they will never speak to you again. At least you will have peaceful nights.

In the majority of cases you will be doing them a favour by pointing out how negative they are. If they realise that you are no longer available as Wailing Wall they might be forced to take action and deal with their problem.

Make sure that you don't just give but also get.

Note: Everyone has rights as well as duties.

If you are only concerned about other people's problems and ignore your own needs and wishes then you are not looking after yourself properly.

People who feel that their own problems are overwhelming them sometimes try to get rid of that pressure by helping others. That way they can avoid having to deal with their own problems and, at the same time, get some social plus points.

Pluck up the courage to lean on others. Ask for a friend's time and attention when you need help. You have the right to receive assistance just like everyone else. It will also make you look more human to others. You may get a lot of admiration and recognition for the efficient way you help others, but it also makes you look like an unattainable person. Someone on a pedestal who seems totally self-sufficient can be a bit scary for others because they may feel they cannot live up to your standards.

SCRIPT

I like myself and others. I deserve the best in life and I am going out to get it. My happiness is important to me. I create my own future. I am on my way to becoming the best possible person I can be. Everything I need for my happiness is already in me. I am complete.

I am a harmonious person. I am in harmony with the world around me. A great sense of serenity spreads through me and I feel calm and relaxed in everything I do. I attract everything that is good like a big magnet. My self-confidence increases every day. I am an attractive person. A great sense of love pervades my being. I love my life and follow my inner voice, which guides me always. My ideal partner is already waiting for me and I will meet him or her in the right place, at the right time.

SHORT FORM

• I am in harmony with myself and the world around me.
  or
  My inner voice guides me always. I am safe.
  or
  My ideal partner is waiting for me. Everything falls into place.

13 | Illness

▼ ▼ ▼ ▼

- I have problems with my stomach.
- I get headaches or backaches frequently.
- I have a benign or malign growth.
- I have problems with my skin.
- I have to go into hospital.

Illnesses are there for a purpose: they are not just a nuisance, they are a warning signal. Unfortunately, most people treat their cars better than they do their own bodies.

When you go along the motorway and the petrol indicator light begins to blink, you go to the nearest petrol station. If the attendant there were to tell you, 'No problem, I'll fix that for you!' and then proceeded to disconnect the light, assuring you that everything was all right now, you would think he was totally mad, and rightly so *because there is nothing wrong with the light, there is something wrong with the petrol level.* If you have a problem with your stomach, the situation is exactly the same. Your body is giving you a warning signal that something is wrong. If you just go and take tablets, then all you are doing is disconnecting the warning light without doing anything about the real problem. You are temporarily 'curing' the symptom, but not the cause.

If you treat your body in this way over a long period of time you will develop further and more serious symptoms because the cause has still not been removed.

One of the problems today is that the medical profession treats only the illness, that is the symptom. Doctors analyse, diagnose, try to find out what illness it is and what drugs they can use to cure it. The *illness* becomes the focal point, and the rest of the person is forgotten. The doctor begins to fight the illness and the patient does not count any more. Listen to doctors in a hospital as they go from ward to ward, discussing their 'cases': the *ulcer* is doing well, and the *appendix* is going home tomorrow.

What if it is the patient who has caused the illness? What if the patient has fallen ill because he or she cannot cope with life?

Illnesses occur when your immune system is down, when you are worried, when you feel hassled, when things are getting you down. This can either happen because you work too hard or because you have been subjected to one or several traumatic events in the past. These can be the death of a relative or close friend, losing your job or getting divorced, to name just a few. Any event that leads to a drastic change in your life-style will exert pressure on you, even if the event is pleasant, like being promoted, getting married or the arrival of a new baby. It is the person who finds it difficult to cope with change who will fall ill.

Worrying, grief, anger, frustration, envy and hatred are all feelings that promote illness. They get the body into overdrive, thus using up energy that is needed to keep the immune system intact, and there is scientific proof that this is so.

In an experiment, a number of volunteers were exposed to cold germs, but only some of them ended up catching a cold. Even though all the subjects had been in the same room, exposed to the same germs, some people stayed well. It turned out that the people who showed resistance to the germs were all those people who reported that they were happy with their lives and felt that they were in control. The people who had fallen ill considered themselves insecure and under constant stress.

These days it is assumed that at least 70 per cent of all illnesses are psychosomatic, meaning that the physical symptoms displayed are expressions of emotional stress. This does not mean that the physical problems are only imaginary, on the contrary. The ulcer, the palpitations, the headaches are very real. The person is not making them up. What the term 'psychosomatic' means is that the *cause* of the illness does not lie in a genetically faulty organ, but that the psyche is out of balance and therefore influences some part of the body in an unfavourable way.

The physical area that is ultimately affected by emotional stress will depend on where we have our weak link or even where we *expect* our weak link to be: 'My father is asthmatic and so is my grandfather, and now I have the same problem. It runs in the family.' We *expect* to develop a certain problem, and our expectations are duly fulfilled. It is actually possible to develop an illness if you just spend enough time thinking about it.

One stage hypnotist demonstrated the working of this rule very effectively. He put a subject under hypnosis and then took a coin out of his purse. He told the subject that he was going to place a very cold piece of metal on his hand and put the coin on the subject's right hand. The subject reported feeling his hand going numb under the 'ice cold' coin. The hypnotist then took the coin away and announced that he was now going to place a red hot piece of metal on the subject's left hand and put the same coin on the subject's other hand. The subject now said he was feeling great heat and a stinging pain in the place where the coin lay. When the hypnotist removed the coin, a blister had formed on the skin.

Fear prepares the ground for susceptibility to physical and mental problems. Being afraid of something means thinking in a negative way about it. The more you fear an illness, the more likely you are to actually attract it.

You get a little understanding of this process when you remember the last time you looked at a medical encyclopedia. You begin to read the text and look at some of the photographs or pictures, and the more you read about the illness, the more worried you get, and then you seem to detect some of the symptoms in yourself. You suddenly notice an itching feeling in your scalp. Is all your hair going to fall out? And then this bruise on your leg. This could be the beginning of a malign growth! This is not to say that in some cases there is not an in-built fault in our genetic make-up where an illness is passed down the line, such as haemophilia or chromosomal abnormalities that affect the development of the foetus, as in Down's Syndrome. The majority of illnesses however are familial rather than inherited or congenital. A familial disease is an illness that you contract simply because you live with a certain group of people, namely your family.

Arthritis is an illness that runs in families and also affects adopted children. Even though they do not have the same genetic material as the rest of the family they develop arthritis. It is now thought that a particularly inflexible and emotionally cold atmosphere promotes the occurrence of arthritis.

Where feelings have to be repressed, the psychological equilibrium is disturbed, and that leads to physical symptoms. The symptoms can even be symbolic of the underlying problem: rigidity of thinking can lead to rigidity of limbs, bottling up of feelings can lead to constipation, inability to express anger outwardly can make it turn inwards and result in depression, reluctance to accept one's femininity can lead to menstrual and sexual problems.

When we feel threatened by an event in the future, we often fall ill. It is a way of avoiding having to deal with the event. You may have noticed that your child develops a temperature or a sore throat on the day a maths test is due. You yourself might feel a headache coming on before you have to go into a difficult meeting. The greater the fear of the coming event, the more severe the symptoms will be. If you feel you cannot cope at all, your nervous system will make sure your body is put out of action for a while.

We are also influenced by past events. A traumatic experience, severe shock or a catastrophic event one or two years beforehand, together with feelings of guilt, fear, and grief, precede the occurrence of cancer and other catastrophic illnesses. Whatever we have not come to grips with emotionally manifests itself physically until we have dealt with the problem or until we die.

The mind can make us *ill*, but the mind can also *heal*. Take this example. Your doctor is sympathetic and prescribes some pills that he assures you are very effective and will help you quickly. You feel better already as you leave his surgery because you expect to get well soon. Your mind has already initiated the healing process. Every time you take a tablet, you think of your doctor's words that these tablets are very effective. It has been shown that people get better because they expect to get better.

When an antidepressant drug was tested in an experiment in a hospital, patients were divided up into two groups. Group A received the new drug, group B was given a placebo (a drug that looks like the real drug, but does not contain any active substances). Neither the doctor nor the patients knew who was receiving the real drug and who was being given the fake one.

At the end of the experiment, group A showed a success rate of 70 per cent, but those in group B, who had received the placebo, *also* showed a 70 per cent success rate. Taking a tablet triggers off the subconscious association of 'getting better', and that is exactly what happens as a consequence.

To take another example, a colleague reported to me that one of his clients suffered from insomnia and was in the habit of taking sleeping tablets every night. One evening she got her tablets mixed up and took a mild laxative instead. She slept soundly through the night, but found that she had diarrhoea the next morning. This happened a couple of times, until she noticed that she had been taking the wrong tablets. She realised that she was obviously capable of sleeping without her pills and so stopped taking them.

Even more remarkable is the case in the United States of a prisoner on death row who chose to have his wrists cut instead of going to the electric chair. He was blindfolded. A warden traced across the prisoner's wrists with a feather and the prisoner died.

We all have this great power of belief in us. Whatever we think about with conviction will come true, no matter whether it is good or bad.

Make sure you know what is going on in your *conscious* mind because that is the only way you can control what is going on in your *subconscious* mind. If you don't run your subconscious mind, somebody else will run it for you and you may get lumbered with things you don't want.

Knowing about the powers of your subconscious mind obliges you to use them. The fact that you have a free will makes you automatically responsible for what is happening to you. It may be bad doing wrong, but it is worse not doing right when you know how to. Not using your knowledge, your time and your talents in a positive way to further your mental and physical health and happiness is possibly the only true sin in this world.

With any illness it is important that you learn to relax. In Part I of this book you encountered a few general exercises to calm your breathing and prepare you for a positive mental attitude. In the following pages I would like to describe a further exercise that is the basis for any positive suggestions you may want to give yourself in order to get well again.

The following exercise is specifically designed to relax you physically. A calm body is a pre-condition for a speedy recovery because when your body is relaxed, skin tension is reduced. In the burns unit of a clinic a number of people were given relaxation treatment under hypnosis once a day over a period of two weeks. It was found that their burns healed in half the time it normally takes. The reduced level of skin tension promoted a decrease in pain, an earlier decrease of inflammation and therefore an acceleration of tissue regeneration.

First of all, decide for yourself where your preferred place of retreat would be. Your sanctuary should be somewhere, real or imagined, where you can feel calm and relaxed. This may be a tropical island, a den in the woods, a cosy room or a garden – it really does not matter, as long as it is idyllic and restful. In the following exercise I have chosen a garden. If you prefer another setting, just change the exercise accordingly. Whenever I refer to breathing I am talking about breathing through your belly (see page 22 for directions on how to do this).

Colour Relaxation

- Make yourself comfortable, sitting or lying down. Make sure your clothes are not too tight. (You may want to open zips or buttons.)
- Close your eyes. Concentrate on outside sounds. Just listen to them. They will be there throughout your relaxation session, but they will not disturb you, rather they will help you to relax even more.
- Now bring your attention into the room, onto yourself. Just be aware of how you are lying there, where your head is, your shoulders, your arms, the trunk of your body, your legs and your feet. Readjust your position if necessary. Make sure you are comfortable.
- Now begin to imagine a staircase, with you standing on the landing looking down. There are ten steps leading down. In your mind, begin to walk down, step by step, counting backwards from ten to zero. Imagine that with every step you walk down you are walking into deeper and deeper relaxation.
- Once you have arrived at the bottom of the steps you will find yourself in front of a wrought iron gate that leads into your special place. The only way of gaining access is by leaving your everyday thoughts outside. Deposit all your problems and worries in a wooden chest that you find by the gate. As soon as you have done so, the gate swings open.

- Now you enter your sanctuary, the place of perfect tranquility. It is a beautiful place, with trees and bushes, flowers and grass, all your favourite things, and it is all yours. The air is sweet, the sun is shining in a brilliant blue sky, the birds are singing and a light breeze makes the temperature just right.
- Find a place somewhere in your garden where you can make yourself comfortable. Lie down and relax.
- Take a deep breath and, as you are breathing out, imagine the colour **red**. As you do, relax your head – the top of your head, your forehead, your eyes and all the muscles around your eyes and your jaw muscles.
- Take another deep breath and, as you are exhaling, imagine the colour **orange**. At the same time, allow your shoulders and arms to go floppy and let your chest muscles relax. You do that by *imagining* that all these parts relax, and they automatically will.
- Take another deep breath. As you breathe out, imagine the colour **yellow**. As you do, let go of any tension in your belly area and your legs. Imagine that all the muscles and fibres become slack and limp and that your whole body is getting so sluggish that it is simply too much trouble to move.
- Take a deep breath again and imagine the colour **green** as you breathe out. Now let your mind come to rest. Any remaining thoughts are now calming down. Don't resist them when you feel them intruding, just let them drift away like little white clouds.
- Now take another deep breath, breathe out and imagine the colour **blue**. Your mental and physical calmness begins to deepen, and you are just sinking deeper and deeper into relaxation.
- Take a deep breath and imagine the colour **lilac** as you exhale. Your mind is completely calm now and a sense of peace pervades your whole being.
- Take another deep breath and imagine the colour **violet** as you breathe out. Tranquility is in every fibre of your body. You have become tranquility. You are now at the centre of your being. You are one with everything around you in your garden, you are part of nature and in harmony with yourself and your environment. You are totally free.

- Stay in this state as long as you wish. When you want to come out of it, just imagine yourself getting up and walking back to the gate. Step outside and close the gate behind you. Then begin to walk up the steps again, counting in your head as you do. When you get to the tenth step, open your eyes again. Remain still for a moment and permit your mind to come back to reality again.

The sense of tranquility and relaxation will stay with you for a while. The more you practise this exercise, the easier and quicker it will be for you to relax. Take the time to do the Colour Relaxation once a day for at least three weeks.

IF YOU HAVE PROBLEMS
Do you find it difficult to imagine the colours?
If you do you may find it helpful to think of objects that are that particular colour, for example, tomatoes, oranges, lemons and so on. Just imagine a whole wall of lemons, say, to get a feel for the colour yellow. If you still find that difficult, look at a yellow object, close your eyes and try to imagine the colour again. Repeat this several times and you will see that your mind begins to form an 'impression' of the colour that you can reproduce when you close your eyes.

Do you find it difficult to deal with any kind of physical interference?
Some people get very irritated if they have to swallow or cough. They may feel that they get an itchy nose or they have to scratch their ear. Don't let these things throw you, and don't let them stop you from continuing with the exercise. If you have to clear your throat, clear it; if you have to scratch your nose, do so. Whatever you do, don't resist these urges because you know that the following is true (remember the Foreword …?)

Note: The harder you try to avoid something, the less you can do it.

The more you try to resist scratching your nose, the more powerful the urge becomes, so just do it straight away. This will help you keep the interference to a minimum. Once you have done the exercise several times, these urges disappear all by themselves. Don't allow trivialities to distract you. The less importance you give to them, the less power they have over you.

Are you having problems with interfering thoughts?

Again, don't put up any resistance. As soon as you catch yourself trailing off to the unrepaired boiler and the school problems of your children, gently (gently!) nudge yourself back to where you left off. If you get stuck in a particular place over and over again, just go on to the next step. Your first objective is to do the exercise at all, your second objective to see it through from beginning to end and only in third place comes the objective to do it well. Just keep at it and you will get better at doing it.

Unless you dedicate a lot of time to meditation, it is unlikely that you will be able to avoid other thoughts drifting through your mind altogether, so just accept them as part of the exercise. They don't really do any harm and will not be detrimental to the relaxing effect of the exercise.

I have problems with my stomach

Do you know what exactly is wrong with your stomach? Do you suffer from heartburn only sometimes or quite frequently? Have you had these problems for a long time?

Please make sure you know what is going on. It is no use trying to ignore the symptoms, hoping that they will just disappear – especially if you have had stomach problems for a long time. You should see your doctor to find out whether it has already developed into something serious or not.

Refusing to look at a problem does not make it go away, so take the first step and face the facts, whatever they may be. You will be better equipped to deal with a problem when you know exactly what it is.

As I noted before, illnesses are warning signals to indicate that there has been a negative chain reaction within the mind-body link, set off by a disharmony in the emotions. Sour thoughts make for a sour stomach.

Be honest with yourself. How many people do you resent at the moment? How many people are you mad at because you feel they have trodden on your toes? How many people do you think are trying to put one over on you in business? If you are not sure about a person, just close your eyes and think of them for a moment. If your stomach reacts you have to put that person on your 'resentment' list. Count the number of people on that list. The more people you can find, the worse your stomach problem is bound to be.

I am not saying that these people are actually trying to do you harm, I am saying that *you think they are*. You may be right about them, but you may just as well be wrong. The more people you think are your enemies the more afraid you get. You begin to feel cornered, and that makes you aggressive or panicky. Your body is prepared for fight or flight, the stomach area contracts, becomes hard, preparing for a potential fist of a potential adversary landing in it. If you then also feed your stomach rich and greasy food, smoke and drink a lot, you are furthering the destructive process. Your stomach cannot work properly to start with because it is in a cramped position and it then has to deal with heavy food and noxious substances as well. An overload situation is inevitable and the stomach begins to send out stronger warning signals.

It gets more and more painful and finally develops an ulcer. You can of course still ignore this, take your tablets, continue to be angry all the time and eat, drink and smoke whatever comes your way. Naturally, the ulcer will become more severe, until it can no longer be kept under control by medication. The next step follows as inevitably as night follows day. Part of your stomach will have to be surgically removed.

I am not trying to scare you. I am just giving you the hard facts of a day in the life of a stressed stomach. By now you will have decided where you personally stand in the hierarchy of stomach problems. From now on it is up to you whether you are going to get better or worse. You have a choice. Remember, even if you do not make a decision, you have still made a decision, namely to get worse. It is not even worth your while continuing reading this chapter.

If you have decided to do something about your stomach problems, you will need to work on two levels. One level is the stress aspect (see pages 66–84). Get your time management sorted out, take breaks, make sure you go on holiday and keep weekends free for your private life. The other level is the physical aspects. Support your body by helping it to relax and so speed up the recovery process. Eat a healthy diet and exercise within reason.

Illness is the absence of health. In order to get well again it is necessary to occupy yourself with health and stop thinking about illness. Thoughts about illness create illness. Thoughts about health create health. Think about the things you want, not about the things you don't want.

Being in hospital makes you feel worse because you are surrounded by objects that make you think of illness – tablets, X-ray machines, syringes, the smell of disinfectant. Some people cannot bear to go and see someone in hospital because these things alone create an acute sense of anxiety in them. How much worse must it be for someone who is forced to go in because of an illness! If it was not for the friendly nurses, it would be a grim prospect indeed.

Health, however, is the normal state, not illness. Yet in spite of all our knowledge, medical research and technical apparatus, health screening and hospitals, we seem to be *less* healthy than ever. This is because we are less *harmonious* than ever. The rat race and competition makes us lose touch with ourselves, our wishes and needs. Just because thousands of people succumb to that destructive life-style, though, does not mean that is the right thing to do. This would be like saying, 'A hundred lemmings throw themselves off a cliff. A hundred lemmings can't be wrong.' Once this imbalance between outer and inner values has been redressed, however, your body will quite naturally go back to its original state of good health.

Here is a way of tackling your stomach problems from the mental side. I assume that you have tried the Colour Relaxation exercise on pages 134–5 by now and have become familiar with your sanctuary. Once you are in your private place of tranquility and your body is reasonably relaxed, continue as follows.

- In your mind, go through your list of people who you hate or fear. Think of every single one and send him or her your best wishes. Sincerely. Forgive them for what they have done to you, even if it is only for the time of your exercise. Be generous, be magnanimous, be a hero, a giant amongst men, but *forgive them.* You are wiser than they are, you can afford this attitude (besides, you want to get rid of your ulcer). This is possibly the most important part of the exercise.
- Begin to concentrate on your stomach area. Initially it might help to put one hand over your stomach.
- Imagine that a bright light (if your image is of the outside world, this can be the sun) shines down on your stomach.

- Imagine your stomach area becoming warmer and warmer, until it is like a little heater within your body, radiating warmth in all directions, into your chest and lungs, into your back and into your belly area, but keep your mind concentrated on your stomach and the feeling of warmth in it. Obviously your hand will create some warmth, but even if you don't put your hand on your belly you can actually create a feeling of warmth by imagining it. Once your stomach feels warm it is relaxing.
- Imagine that you can make yourself very small, smaller and smaller until you are so tiny you can get inside your stomach and walk around in it.
- Picture your stomach. You may visualise it as a den or a cave (anatomical accuracy is of no importance here). Imagine the walls dripping with moisture. This is the excess acid that is causing you the stomach problems.
- See yourself going around your stomach with a big soft sponge that is highly absorbent and imagine yourself softly dabbing up all the excess acid from the walls and the floor. Go into every corner. Be thorough.
- Once you have completed this task, imagine a velvety material that is very soft, and begin to clad the inside of your stomach with it. Imagine how soothing it would feel to have a silky soft protective layer lining your stomach.
- Now leave your stomach. Imagine how you are becoming your normal size again. Take your mind back to your sanctuary. Relax for a moment after the work you have done, then leave your sanctuary again, going back the way you came.
- When you close the gate behind you, drop that sponge in the wooden casket by the gate. Keep your sanctuary tidy!

Do this exercise regularly. Once you have learnt to relax more quickly you can go through the initial sequences more swiftly. You will not have to go through the whole colour range because your subconscious mind will have learnt to associate the colour violet with deep relaxation, so it will be enough to just think of violet to get into that state. The graver your stomach problems are, the more frequently you should do this exercise.

One part that you should never ever leave out or cut down on is that of forgiving. I cannot emphasise enough how important this part is. You will see the most amazing results and find that it creates the most pleasant positive side-effects. I see it over and over again in clients who apply this method. They suddenly get on with the people they thought were their enemies. This is because when you think well of someone and send them your best wishes, you change your attitude. You become more relaxed about that person, and that will show. Instead of getting angry you will laugh. The other person feels more relaxed with you and may find that there is no need to be aggressive or cold or haughty any longer.

Always remember that aggression and contempt are signs of fear and lack of self-confidence. Others may be afraid of you because you are so strict, serious and demanding. By changing your attitude towards others you give them and yourself a better chance to get on in harmony and everyone is happy. Show what a great person you really are deep down inside. Be a hero, take the leap into positive thinking. You can only win.

I get headaches or backaches frequently

Your first step, again, is to find out a bit more about those aches. Keep a diary and make a note of what has been happening shortly before or after the pains occur. Sometimes it can be an allergy to chocolate, cheese or wine that creates headaches. Another reason for headaches or backaches can be the wrong posture, bad seating or an occupation that puts a lot of strain on the spine or the eyes, for example typing or writing for hours on end.

These are things you can remedy easily. There is no need to put up with a lousy chair at work if it gives you backaches. You have a right to have proper tools for your job, and a good chair is one of them. Insist on it. Tell your boss that you want to do good work, but you can only do so if you get appropriate seating. If you don't look after your health, no one else will.

Head- and backaches are not always triggered off by nutritional or mechanical problems. Read through your diary carefully. Does your neck or back ache every time after you had to deal with a particular situation at work? Do your headaches turn up every time you have to do something you are afraid of? Trite as it may sound, do you develop a headache every time your husband wants sex?

Fear is at the bottom of every illness. Fear makes you seize up. Your body goes rigid, you are 'scared stiff'. The tension that this creates shows itself as pain.

You may feel that you are not getting the moral or emotional support you need, that no one 'backs you up', and that hurts. At the same time you may feel too weak to take control of the situation. You lack the strength and the 'backbone' to stand up for yourself.

Let us assume that you have regular meetings with your boss on Friday afternoons to keep him or her informed about the progress of a particular project. Let us further assume that you always end up with an aching back after these meetings. You put one and one together and conclude that it is your boss and the fact that you have to report to him or her that causes your backaches. But when you look more closely at the sequence of events, you will see that the trouble starts at a much earlier point in time. As you know that you will have to go in every Friday, you have time to mentally prepare yourself for it, and this is when the die is cast. Check up on this now. Close your eyes and think of the next meeting with your boss. If you feel comfortable with the thought, your body will not react. If you are afraid of that meeting, you will notice a physical reaction in the form of muscular tension. The degree of this tension will depend on the degree of your fear. When the tension reaches a certain threshold, it is translated into a particular physical symptom. This can be, amongst other things, a stomach-ache, headache, backache or neckache. Instead of saying that your *boss* is a pain in the neck, you should really be saying that you are giving *yourself* a pain in the neck. It is not the meeting as such that produces the physical symptom, it is your way of thinking about the situation that will decide whether you feel ill afterwards or not.

Monitor your thoughts about these meetings. They may well start as early as the Tuesday or Wednesday. What is going through your mind when you think of Friday? Let me guess. It is something like, 'I haven't been able to reach the contractor this week. I just haven't had time to chase him up. My boss won't like that' or, 'I'm not sure whether I have made the right decision. Maybe I should have double-checked with my boss before I gave production the go ahead' or, 'God, he is in such a foul mood today. I don't know how I can face him tomorrow to tell him that we didn't get the job we tendered for!', or, 'I did my very best, but I wasn't able to negotiate a better contract with the client. I'm worried that my boss will think I'm a failure.' You are worried, you are anxious, you see yourself as an under-achiever, and, hey presto, your nervous system follows suit and switches into gloom-and-doom mode. By thinking fearfully you have set the course of events to 'negative'. Notice, though, how all these unpleasant physical feelings dissolve into thin air when you find out that your boss does not want to deal with that contractor any more, so it suddenly does not matter that you could not get hold of him.

Don't let self-doubt get the upper hand. Difficulties can arise at any point in time while you are working on a project. As long as you do your level best to deal with them, you have nothing to reproach yourself for.

Don't let yourself or others accuse you of being inefficient when you know you are not. Stand by the decisions you made. There are always several ways in which you can deal with a problem, so you need to select the one that appears most suitable at the time. Explain why you took that particular course of action, but don't apologise for it.

Some people find that their headaches start every time they are faced with an unpleasant chore. One of my clients developed migraine-like headaches whenever she had to go and see her husband's relatives. It turned out that she felt threatened because her in-laws were professionally highly qualified and looked down on her.

On further examination it turned out that my client felt resentful towards her in-laws 'for having had it better in life' than she had, and she therefore refused to talk to them. Every attempt by the in-laws to talk to her was immediately blocked by her. She would either ignore the other person or reply in an abrupt manner. Gradually the family began to reduce their attempts to communicate with her, which she readily interpreted as the in-laws being stuck up. She saw her worst fears come true. Once the idea had firmly settled in her mind that her new relatives despised her, she began to feel more and more anxious about going to see them. She also got into arguments with her husband who reproached her for being antisocial and paranoid. When she started having headaches every time she was due to visit her in-laws, it was not all bad.

Somewhere deep down it was also a relief because now she had an excuse for not going.

She found it quite hard to let go of her feelings of envy, but she was an intelligent lady who came to understand that it was her own inferiority complex that had triggered off the unpleasant atmosphere during her visits as well as her headaches. Once she recognised what lay at the bottom of her problem, she was able to change her attitude and the headaches vanished. She is now getting on well with her in-laws and is looking forward to her visits.

If you suffer from lack of self-confidence, you doubt yourself. You doubt that you are capable of achieving your targets, you doubt that you will succeed. Doubt makes you hesitate when you should be sure; it makes you give up when you should press forward. Doubt is counterproductive. Don't waste time on doubt, begin to believe. Believe that you will make it, believe yourself to death rather than waste one more minute doubting yourself.

Note: Believe in yourself.

You are unique. You are important. There is a place in the world that only you can fill and nobody else. Go for the best. Why drive when you can fly? Make sure you are using all your abilities to their best advantage. Make sure your life is happy. The more self-confidence you can develop the easier it will be for you to reach your goals.

Self-confidence is not the same thing as conceit. A conceited person boasts about his own achievement in a way that makes you wonder what that person could do with a loaf and two fishes, but, in reality, he is unsure of himself or cannot acknowledge other people's achievements. A confident person, on the other hand, has no need to belittle others, on the contrary: he can feel pleasure at seeing other people thrive, safe in the knowledge that he is successful in his own way. Envy and jealousy become superfluous once you start believing in yourself.

Developing headaches when sex looms large is basically very similar to the above example of my lady client and her in-laws. Again, negative thoughts of fear lie at the bottom of the headaches and the sexual problems.

As we saw in the chapter on Stress, pages 66–84, sex is only possible when you are relaxed. If, for any reason, you consider sex immoral, a chore, a threat or something shameful then your subconscious mind will prevent it. Your body will react to your negative thoughts and 'close up', making intercourse painful or impossible. This, of course, helps to reinforce your preconceptions of sex as being unpleasant and next time the same thing happens again. You will come to hate and detest sex, and the headaches will begin to occur regularly.

Many women do not know themselves very well when it comes to their own bodies. They were brought up to think that their body was somehow dirty and that they therefore should wash regularly. Whatever happens 'down there' was rarely discussed between mother and daughter. Periods and pregnancy were dealt with in the briefest of terms and that is where their sex education ground to a halt. By the time a girl in such a situation has her first period, she has already understood that genitals are not to be discussed and that any further questions are only going to be met with embarrassed silence. Any physical pleasure that is remotely sexual is coupled with a feeling of doing wrong. It is not surprising that, in such an atmosphere, the sexual act evokes even greater feelings of guilt in the adult woman.

It is ignorance that promotes fear of sex. Because the girl's genitals are ignored the girl realises that they are a taboo area where you are not supposed to look. When she touches herself she does it secretly, sometimes without actually knowing which part of her genitals it is that gives her this pleasurable feeling. Many women don't know anything about their own timing, what sort of stimulation they prefer and where their erogenous zones lie, let alone what they want from a man during intercourse.

It is not really that difficult to catch up on that lack of knowledge. You are an adult now. Give yourself permission to look at your body in the mirror. Take in all the details. Take your time over it. This is your body and it is important that you know exactly what it looks like.

- Look at your arms and legs, the shape of your shoulders and breasts, your waist and your hips. Look at yourself from all sides and angles. Get used to the shape of your body. Repeat this exercise every day until you feel

comfortable doing it. You are not doing anything weird, you are learning about yourself.
- Take a small mirror and look at your genitals. There is no need to feel guilty, on the contrary. It is high time you know what this part of your body looks like.

Sex is fun and it is a perfectly normal thing to do – no matter what your mother told you. She has been wrong before, hasn't she? Sex is part of life and creates happiness and, as such, it is a vital ingredient to self-fulfilment. If you have hang-ups about sex, then do something about them. As with every other achievement, you will have to be patient. It takes time to change negative attitudes. Just persist, and slowly you will perceive changes occurring, as improbable as it may seem at the moment.

Once you know yourself and your own body better, you may find that you have needs that are not fulfilled by your partner. If he is doing things you don't like, stop him. If he is doing things that are ineffective, tell him – nicely. *Don't* pull out your magazine from under the bed and start reading to indicate that you are not turned on by what he is doing. Tact is essential in bed, but talking is not prohibited. Say what you want, but say it without accusing or offending, otherwise you are creating stress for your partner and by now we know what consequences that has on sexual performance …

If there is something you would like him to do, either try and guide him by gently pushing him or leading his hand, or say what you want. Remember that he cannot do something for you when he does not know that you want it.

Maybe you want to explain to him beforehand that you want to try out some new things. That way he is prepared for alterations in your mutual sexual routine and can react more easily to your wishes.

Note: It is OK to say what you want.

That goes for every area in life and does not exclude sex.

SCRIPT

I feel free. I am filled with harmony and love. I love myself and my body.
I take pride in my body and, as I am getting to know it, I feel better every
day. I feel more and more positive about myself. I leave my past behind and
start a new life. I enjoy my new-found freedom and look to the future with
confidence. My self-confidence grows daily. I notice with delight how
beautiful my body is. It makes me happy to know that a new area of life
opens to me now.

SHORT FORM

- Getting to know myself is important to me. I love my body and enjoy its
  beauty.

I have a benign or malignant growth

It is a very upsetting experience to discover that you have a lump somewhere in
your body that should not be there. You may detect it by chance or you may
find out about it during a routine check-up. Wherever it is, the first thought
that springs to mind is 'cancer', and that is *very* frightening indeed. I speak
from experience, because it happened to me at a young age. When I was
seventeen, I discovered a lump in my right breast. I was horrified. I went to my
doctor who examined me and recommended that I have the lump removed and
analysed. She thought that the growth would probably turn out to be benign,
but she did not want to run any risks.

In spite of her reassurances I still felt anxious. I was worried about the
operation and how it would affect the shape of my breast. How big would the
scar be? Would that breast be smaller than the other one after the operation?
All these questions seem trivial when you consider that I might have been
seriously ill with cancer, but that possibility seemed at times more remote than
the more immediate fears about the mutilating effects of the operation.

I went in for the operation, which was done under local anesthetic in 20
minutes. I was allowed home immediately afterwards and, a few days later, to
my great relief, received the message that the growth was benign. The wound
healed well and left a scar that is now hardly visible.

Fifteen years later, I discovered another lump, but this time it was really big, at least three times the size of the first one. Although I knew that, as the first one had been benign, the next one was, in all probability, also going to be benign, I was scared at the size. If they were going to remove *this* lump it would mean taking half my breast away and I would be a cripple.

For a few weeks I could not even face consulting my doctor about it. I was just too scared of the consequences. I finally managed to pick up enough courage to go and see her. When she had examined my breast she confirmed that the chances of this growth being malignant were minimal and that she therefore saw no reason for removing the lump for the time being. I was relieved on the one hand, but still felt that I was carrying around some sort of time bomb in my body that could turn into a malign growth any time. I wanted to get rid of it, but not at the price of losing half my breast.

I then commenced to fight the growth mentally. I decided that this lump was an unwelcome addition to my body that I did not want. I imagined that the growth was a black rubbish bag. In my mind, I kicked it hard, over and over again, until it detached itself from the ground and eventually rolled down into a sewage canal where it was swept away.

This image made me laugh because I come from a family where you do not kick rubbish bags around, certainly not when you are a girl. It was a bit like rebelling against my parents, and I quite enjoyed that feeling. I kicked that rubbish bag over and over again in my mind and, after a few weeks, I noticed that the growth had diminished in size. I continued my fantasy for another two weeks and the growth was gone. Without knowing it at the time, I had employed a Positive Thinking technique.

Of course I have no way of scientifically proving that it was my efforts that effected the change. Maybe the lump would have disappeared all by itself. It is a fact, however, that your thinking influences what goes on in your body. Today we have the technical means of showing unambiguously that the blood chemistry in the body undergoes changes that can be directed at will by the things we imagine. Biofeedback machines, for example, can be used to teach a person to control their blood-pressure, heart rate or production of stomach acids, that is, control responses that are not normally under voluntary control.

To control blood-pressure, the client is connected to the biofeedback machine and asked to let his or her mind drift. The moment the client's blood-pressure falls below a specific level, a light begins to flash. This provides immediate feedback for the client who can then analyse what he or she is thinking when the blood-pressure is low and can then repeat that thought to keep it low.

Positive Thinking also influences the functioning of the brain. This can be measured on an electroencephalogram (EEG), which records the pattern of minute electric waves emitted by the brain. While you are meditating or going through your relaxation exercises, changes in brain wave patterns occur. The brain produces alpha waves, which are similar to rhythms emitted during sleep and more regular than waves produced during normal waking states.

When thoughts provoke strong emotions, the physical consequences are even more striking. Two sisters, aged eight and ten, were left in a room with a one-way mirror screening them off from their parents who were in the room next door. The girls could observe their parents, but the parents could not see the girls.

Both children suffered from diabetes – the older girl severely, the younger one only lightly. While the children were watching their parents next door, their blood chemistry was monitored. When the parents started rowing the girls' blood chemistry changed so dramatically that even the younger sister suffered temporarily from severe diabetes. The higher levels were maintained for a long time after the row the girls saw between the parents was over.

Knowledge about this close link between the mind and the body has led to the development of strategies that enable sufferers to influence their body in a beneficial manner and thus help combat their illness. Cancer clinics have been using these techniques for quite a number of years, and some of the results are amazing.

You personally may decide to go for conventional therapy such as radiation treatment and chemotherapy and only in addition employ the mental strategies. Whatever your decision, you owe it to yourself to support conventional treatment by strengthening your physical defence mechanism by employing the powers of your subconscious mind. Mobilise your inner forces. Bring your body back into a state of harmony.

- Make sure you know what the state of affairs is. Do not ignore a growth – consult a specialist to find out what it is.
- Make sure you get all the information you can about various forms of treatment. Find out what side-effects you will have to expect, because forewarned is forearmed.
- Begin to do relaxation exercises at once. They will help you get over any possible unpleasant side-effects more easily and your immune system will work more efficiently.
- Find a symbol for your growth. Imagine it as an object. In my case it was a black rubbish bag, but you may see it as a stained surface that needs scrubbing off or a big boulder that is in the way or a layer of thick material that needs to be peeled off bit by bit to let your skin underneath breathe freely again.
- Decide how you would want to remove the growth. How would you tackle that growth in your lungs or this patch on your skin? You could scrub it away, you could chisel it off, you could shoot at it so that it cracks and finally crumbles away. You could trample it into little pieces and then carry the bits off and throw them into the sea.
- Find some physical activity that appears effective to you. Whatever activity it is, it has to be satisfying and elating. It has to leave you with a sense of achievement. Do not choose a mode of attack that makes you feel annoyed because that would disturb the healing process.
- If you think you would like the support from others in your imagery, invent some helpers. They could be giants or bouncers, real people or fantasy figures. Integrate them into your combat strategy, see them helping you in your efforts to destroy the growth.

Let us assume that you have chosen to see that patch on your lung as a great black block of concrete and you want to use hammer and chisel to destroy it. This is what you do.

- First of all relax. This is of the utmost importance because it helps your body get into an equilibrium, and that in itself has a healing effect.

- Imagine that big black block right there in front of you. Imagine yourself strong as Hercules. See yourself picking up hammer and chisel. Start at one end of the block and hammer away. See the first cracks appear, see the first chips come off and fall to the ground. Continue until the whole block is smashed up.
- In your mind, snap your fingers and make the rubble disappear. Have a big lorry carry it away and dump it on a rubbish tip or make a torrent of rain wash it away.
- Feel a sense of satisfaction in your achievement. Feel proud of yourself.
- Repeat this exercise *at least* ten times a day. At least! In addition, you can help yourself by reading the following script.

Script

My body is strong and healthy. All my muscles and organs work in perfect harmony. Love fills my whole being and dissolves anything that is detrimental to my health. My whole body is filled with peace and harmony, from the tips of my toes to the top of my head. Health and well-being fill every cell of my body. The love I feel inside me is so powerful that it takes over my whole being. I am filled with harmony. I create harmony. I am harmony.

Short Form

- Every cell of my body is filled with love and harmony. The growth dissolves. I am healthy.

I have problems with my skin

Skin problems like acne, eczema or psoriasis indicate that there is an imbalance in your metabolism. Your metabolism is influenced by what you eat, but also by how you cope with life in general.

First of all, check what you are eating. Are you on an eat-as-many-packets-of-crisps-as-you-can-and-swill-it-all-down-with-a-couple-of-cans-of-Coke diet with a few bars of chocolate afterwards to fill any remaining gaps in your stomach?

I am sure you realise that this sort of food is not only unhealthy, it also clogs up your metabolism in a way that prevents your digestion from working properly. Substances that should be excreted are no longer discharged, they remain in the body, but they have to go somewhere, so they come out in the skin.

It depends on the individual to what extent their eating habits affect them. Some people can eat chocolate all day long without showing any adverse effects on their skin, whereas others only have to look at a piece of cake to come out in spots. So why is there this difference between people?

We have seen in previous chapters that the workings of the body are dependent on what we put in. This does not only mean food, but also the type of mental nourishment we give it. The quality of our thoughts will determine how healthy we are. Positive thoughts create positive emotions and, ultimately, good health. Negative thoughts and emotions 'constipate' the mind just as much as the body. If you are emotionally well-balanced, you are healthy. Your mental equilibrium keeps your body functioning perfectly so that junk food is dealt with easily, provided it does not arrive in vast quantities.

Interestingly, it is not the emotionally stable people who go for large quantities of fatty or sweet food, it is people who have emotional problems. This suggests that eating habits are dependent on your state of mind. This also explains why people find it easy to stick to a diet when they are happy, but find it nearly impossible when they feel low.

If you compare your digestive system to a vessel with a drainage that only opens when you are relaxed, then you could say that balanced people keep their outlet working and therefore can afford to pour unhealthy substances down, whereas unbalanced people accumulate poisonous substances in a vessel that has an obstructed outlet. The level of poison gradually rises higher until it spills over the top of the vessel. That is when you come out with rashes, eczema and other skin problems.

Your metabolism can also be disturbed by stress. When you are tense all the time, your body cannot function properly. Your digestion suffers not because of harmful input, but because of a physical inability to work normally. A tensed up stomach cannot function normally and neither can tensed up bowels.

The skin is the reflection of the soul. It is the outward projection screen that shows what film is playing inside. When you are not in harmony with yourself, when you do not like yourself, your skin will show this.

Apart from the hormonal changes that occur at that time, fear of one's own sexuality can sometimes be the cause for acne during puberty. You are trying to suppress a feeling that frightens you because it is new and powerful. You are trying to prevent it from taking over but you can't. It cannot be held back, so it comes out in your skin.

Eczema is a disorder that can occur as a consequence of being degraded and put down. Humiliating someone else stems from having been humiliated yourself when you were young. You can only pass on what you know and if love and understanding are not part of your emotional vocabulary then you cannot speak the language of love. Derision is the weapon of an emotionally impotent person. If you put someone down, you make them feel small and you make them feel ashamed, but you also create hatred and opposition in that person because you are destroying their dignity. This is why humiliating someone to teach him or her a lesson or to make him or her stop doing something does not work. In order to get someone's co-operation you have to negotiate with them in a manner that is acceptable to both sides. You may force a child to stop hitting his little brother by humiliating him, but the moment your back is turned the child will do the same thing again. So you have not really taught your child anything, on the contrary. Because the child's dignity has been damaged it feels out of control and powerless. In order to restore his self-respect he had to prove to himself that he does have some power left, and the only person weaker than himself is his little brother who is the last one in the pecking order. Now the little brother has to be hit as a matter of principle.

Feelings of being helplessly subjected to a bullying parent lead to aggression, frustration and fear. As you are not supposed to hate your parents, children feel guilty about their negative feelings towards them and this creates ongoing inner conflict: the child wants to love the parent but is rejected, the child feels angry but cannot show it if it wants to ensure the parent's love. No matter what the child does, it is going to be wrong.

If you have been brought up under these sorts of conditions then let me say the following:

- other people have to *earn* your love
- no one has an automatic right to your love
- this goes for your parents just as much as for anybody else.

Just because your parents are your parents does not mean that they can abuse you and still expect to be loved. *You are not neurotic just because you don't like being kicked around.*

Inner conflicts create tension and that tension has to be released in one way or another. If your skin is your weak point, then it is here where the tension will surface.

Script

I am a strong and positive person. I am courageous and I am safe in the knowledge that the core of my personality is healthy and invulnerable. Nothing disturbs me. I love myself and others. I accept myself and I am open to new things. I welcome my sexuality as part of my person.

I am whole. I am healthy and happy. I can see my skin soft and clean and clear. A great sense of tranquility spreads through my entire body and dissolves any tension. My positive mental attitude promotes the healing process. My skin reflects my new attitude. I am calm and relaxed. I feel love and happiness spreading through my body and mind. My skin is clear.

Short Form

- I am strong and positive. My mind is filled with tranquility and my skin is healthy.

  or

  The core of my being is intact. My skin is clear.

I have to go into hospital

Going into hospital has two sides to it: it can be frightening, but, for some, it can also be desirable. It can be an escape from the stresses and strains of everyday life. Hospital can be a place of refuge, just as the illness that got you there in the first place can be a refuge.

Physical problems are always a sign of emotional disharmony. When you don't live your feelings, you create tension. Tension produces aggression and if this is not released in one way or another it is turned inside and mental or physical illness ensues.

Many physical problems have been set up subconsciously to protect the sufferer from something. A woman who binges constantly may be unhappy about her weight and about being unattractive, but what an excellent wall of defence she has now to avoid having to have a sexual relationship with a man! She will find it quite impossible to go on a diet and lose some of that weight, simply because subconsciously she does not really want to.

At the opposite end of this spectrum we find anorexia. Although it constitutes the exact opposite of bingeing, it can serve exactly the same purpose. By starving the body, any traces of femininity are kept to an absolute minimum. The thinner the body, the smaller the breasts and the smaller the danger of attracting attention from the opposite sex.

Illness can also be a way of attracting attention to yourself. As a child, you may have experienced the satisfaction of your mother fussing over you when you were ill. You had friends visiting you, received little presents, the cat was allowed on the bed and you had your favourite meals cooked for you. You learnt that being ill had its rewards and you have not forgotten that. So now when problems get on top of you and you have not learnt to deal with them in an adult manner, you will subconsciously choose another way out. You develop an illness and, unless you change your attitude to life, this can land you in hospital where you are relieved of all responsibility. Whatever happens to you from now on is up to the doctors – or so you think.

Being in hospital you have a lot of time on your hands. Use that time wisely. Begin to practise relaxation, regularly. Once you are back home you may not have that time. You are being given a unique opportunity to change your way of looking at things.

Start filling your mind with the results you wish to achieve. Don't squander any time on thinking about problems you may encounter on your way to your goal. If you have had a stroke and you cannot move your left arm and leg, see yourself back at home, playing ball with your children, easily using both arms, running around effortlessly. If you have problems with your lungs, picture yourself breathing deeply and effortlessly. No one can force you to give in to frightening thoughts, so if you don't like them, replace them with constructive ones of health and happiness. As soon as you catch yourself drifting off into thoughts of gloom and doom, cut them off and stamp a positive image of health over them. *Insist* on getting better. Keep your goal in mind – always.

Stop blaming others for what happened to you. Tidy up any emotional junk you are carrying around with you. Throw out resentment, hate and envy. Open yourself to others, make a point of looking for their good sides. Decide to like yourself and others from now on. Forgive yourself and others for anything that happened in the past and make a fresh start. Push back old barriers and make room for amazing new possibilities. Surprise yourself.

Allow the real you to emerge now, that truly superior person you know you really are. Cast off any emotional burdens you have been carrying all these years – they are not part of the real you and only hold you back. Look at yourself as strong and positive, see yourself as the creator of your own destiny, be it for health, wealth or happiness.

If you have to undergo an operation, make yourself a tape that you can play during the operation as well as afterwards during the recovery period (see the Script on page 157). Some hospitals have already started using this method. While the operation is in progress, the patient is played a tape over headphones. The tape contains messages for a speedy recovery that the subconscious mind registers even though the patient is anaesthetised. It has been shown that patients who have been played these tapes recover more quickly and suffer less from nausea and depression after the operation.

Don't be put off by pessimistic prognoses. Just because your doctor does not see a way does not mean you won't get better. It just means that he has exhausted his methods. There are a great many examples of people who the doctors had given up on but who recovered nevertheless.

One man was told that he had another two months to live. When he heard his death sentence he did not say anything for a while and then he started to laugh. He suddenly realised how ridiculously insignificant all the things were that he had spent all his life worrying about. Everyone thought he had gone crazy with despair. The man went home and began to live a new life. He shifted his priorities from worrying to enjoying – and recovered completely. The doctors could not give an explanation for his recovery.

As long as you don't give up, you can recover. You carry the strongest remedy inside yourself: your belief in your recovery. 'According to your faith be it done unto you', as it says in the Bible. What you have to do is to fire that belief system with positive power and leave the rest to nature. As usual, your subconscious mind will faithfully carry out what you send down in the form of images.

Pictures of health produce health. You attract the things you give a great deal of thought to. Your words are the open sesame that dissolve obstacles and remove barriers. Your thoughts are the way to moving mountains.

SCRIPT
My body is filled with health and strength. My mind is focused on recovery, my thoughts are filled with optimism and happiness. From now on I spend a lot of time thinking of my aims. The natural healing forces in me set to work now, harmonising my whole being, generating an enormous amount of energy that helps me reach my goal. I can see myself quite clearly as a healthy person, enjoying my life. My positive thoughts attract all that is good and healthy. I recover quickly and easily. I give thanks that I am well again.

SHORT FORM
- I recover quickly and easily. I have faith in the healing powers of my mind. I am divinely protected.

14 | Jealousy and Envy

▼ ▼ ▼ ▼

- When I see my girlfriend talking with another man I get really upset.
- I find myself ugly. I envy all these other women who are so beautiful.
- It bothers me immensely that my husband is driving a smaller car than his colleagues.
- We have an open relationship, but I find I cannot cope with my girlfriend having affairs.
- I am a second wife. I am jealous of my husband's first family because he gives them a lot of attention.

You are jealous when you seek to possess another person. Jealousy has nothing to do with love, it has to do with wanting to cement your brittle ego by procuring the undivided attention of your partner. The partner becomes the love dispenser, and the jealous person can only be happy when they receive attention around the clock, but even then, it is not enough.

A jealous person is totally egotistical and not at all interested in the needs of their partner. They think they love their partner because they fuss so much over them, but their behaviour has very little to do with caring. They don't trust their partner and always suspect an affair behind every late return from the office.

In extreme cases, a person will go to any lengths to find out what their partner is up to. They are obsessed with the thought that their partner might find someone more attractive than them and leave them, so they check their partner's clothes, briefcase, correspondence, check whether he or she is in the office, ring the house at night when they go out to see whether he or she is in. They might even engage a private detective to follow him or her around. Even if the detective assures them that nothing has happened, they don't believe it. Such is their inferiority complex that they cannot believe their partner will want to stay with them. No amount of talking will convince them of their partner's loyalty, and all the attention in the world will not put their mind at ease. They are a bottomless vessel that you can fill with love and understanding day-in, day-out and the only result you get is that you have to start from scratch the day after.

The consequence of such behaviour is obvious. You reap what you sow. Confronting another person with suspicions will make the suspicions come true. As your partner finds it impossible to convince you of his or her innocence, he or she will finally go off and really have an affair. At least now your accusations are true. If you want to destroy a relationship, then jealousy is a sure way of doing just that.

Envy is a bit similar to jealousy, with the difference that it concerns other people's possessions or circumstances that you consider to be bigger, better, more expensive, or trendier than your own. Happiness is not only dependent on the possession of certain prestigious objects, it is also dependent on being seen to be the one person who has the best. This is how the game of 'keeping up with the Joneses' was invented. Envy is dependent on the presence of others. It cannot exist on a desert island with only one inhabitant.

It is not even a matter of *needing* a four-wheel-drive lawnmower, but you simply cannot bear to see the neighbour whizz past with his. It makes you sick to detect, as you believe, this superior smile on his face as he is cutting his grass.

If you suffer from envy, you are probably an 'if only' person: 'if only I had a bigger salary I would be happy', 'if only I had a bigger house I would be happy'. No you wouldn't, because as soon as your friends caught up, you would have to start if-onlying again. Envy puts you into a no-win position because it is always easy to find someone else who has a bigger, better, newer whatever than you.

You can also envy someone else's life-style. Your friend goes out almost every night because she is single. You cannot because you are married and have to look after the children. Is that maybe why you don't protest when you hear someone make a disparaging remark about your single friend's life-style? A lot of bickering is nothing but sour grapes.

Jealousy and envy are prime destroyers of relationships. They are poisons that cloud the mind and distort perception. They have usually been copied from parents and originate in a fundamental lack of self-confidence that needs to be balanced out by accumulating possessions, either of objects or of people.

When I see my girlfriend talking with another man I get really upset

A young man of 26, let us call him John, came to see me because he felt that his jealousy was jeopardising his relationship with his girlfriend. This was not the first time that this had occurred – his previous two relationships had ended in disaster because of his own attitude, as he admitted.

He told me that he felt all right when he started going out with a girl because he felt still reasonably detached at that stage, but, after a while, the old problem would creep back and he would resent her spending time with her friends, even if he was invited to join them. It became even worse when she wanted to spend some time on her own or when she was speaking to another man. His immediate thought was that she did not want him any more.

He was pushing very hard to see her daily to reassure himself that she was still interested in him. As he was at her place almost every day and she did not want to neglect her friends, she invited them around, but that again made him feel left out. He felt cornered and confused. On the one hand the girl told him that she loved him, but on the other hand, he felt he was detecting contradictory messages because he was not always the centre of her attention. He realised that his jealousy was at the bottom of his troubles and declared he would like to save the relationship and that he was quite prepared to change if only he knew how.

He felt quite helpless in situations that aroused his jealousy. It was almost as if he was watching a film that he had seen hundreds of times. He knew the sequences by heart and there did not seem to be a way of stopping his feelings from running away with him. His jealousy seemed to have become a thing in itself, outside of his control.

The most important piece of information so far is that John thought that his girlfriend might 'not want him any more' whenever she gave her attention to other people, particularly other men. With this sentence John gave me the key to the problem. The message he was receiving from his subconscious mind was that, whenever he started getting fond of someone, he was in danger of being rejected. The more involved he got, the greater the fear of being rejected became and the harder he tried to hold on to the girl.

As we have seen in the chapter about the subconscious mind in Part I, these messages have their origin in the past, so, when John and I began to talk about his childhood, it turned out that John's parents had given him and his little brother away to a foster family when he was very young because they both had to work to support the family and did not have time to look after the children. When they felt financially secure after five years they went to collect the children to take them back home. By that time, of course, the children had got used to their foster family and did not want to leave. They yelled and screamed, but they were told they had to leave with those people they did not really know and they were finally forced away.

This traumatic experience, together with all the feelings of fear and anxiety of having to leave the beloved foster parents, were imprinted on John's mind at that early age. Because children always blame themselves for what happens to them, John subconsciously assumed that he must be unlovable for his foster parents to allow him to be taken away by people he hardly knew. John loved his foster parents, but it seemed to him that they rejected him because there was something wrong with him. This feeling was later reinforced by his own father who, angry at not being loved and accepted by his son, told him he was bad and beat him terribly for the slightest of reasons.

John's trust in people and in himself had been nearly completely destroyed by that time. Even after he had left his family, history seemed to repeat itself. His lack of self-confidence attracted girls who lacked self-confidence themselves and who could not help his ego to heal. Also, his jealous behaviour made them feel oppressed so that all they wanted to do in the end was to get away from him. Or they ended up going off with someone else, making John's worst fears come true.

It took John a long time to find his way out of these complicated feelings, but he managed to do so in the end, thanks to his own efforts. He has now been with his girlfriend for two years and is getting on well.

SCRIPT

- I am a lovable person. I am attractive and other people enjoy being with me. I trust myself and my abilities, I believe that I am lovable. My belief makes me strong and it is this inner strength that allows me to trust my partner. I enjoy this relationship and I find it easy to allow my partner to express him or herself freely. I am happy to see my partner at ease and carefree. My self-confidence helps our partnership to thrive. I am easy-going and happy.

SHORT FORM

- I am self-confident and easygoing. I trust myself and my partner.

I find myself ugly. I envy all these other women who are so beautiful

This thinking happens for two reasons. Either you have just been left by your lover, or your parents or some other people in your childhood gave you the impression that you were ugly and you have believed this ever since.

When you think you are getting on well with your partner and he suddenly leaves you, then this is a considerable blow to your ego. As far as you are concerned everything was alright, until one day you get home and find a note to say that he is not coming back because he found someone else or that he does not want to commit himself (which in some cases can be another way of saying that he has found someone else).

After the initial shock, you begin to ask yourself what you have done wrong. You always got on, there were never any serious arguments, he never complained about anything and yet he has just left you. And now you switch into child-mode – ('it must be me!') – which constitutes a temporary regression into your early years. In spite of glaring evidence to the contrary, you blame yourself. You reproach yourself for having been so naive as to think that you could hold a man like him with your inferior looks. You hate going out into the street and seeing all those pretty young girls whose good looks have never bothered you before. But now you feel rejected and you look at them with different eyes. You look at them with the eyes of your ex-partner and, every time you see another woman, you involuntarily ask yourself whether this is the type your ex-partner prefers to you, whether these are the sort of looks that turn him on. It appears suddenly that the whole town is overpopulated with beautiful swans and you are the only ugly duckling in the pond.

You may be miserable, but this is nothing compared with someone who has considered herself ugly all her life. The moment you have a new partner you perk up again, dismissing all your previous negative thoughts about your looks and going back to thinking that you are attractive, but when you have been brought up with the idea that you don't look like much, that there isn't anything that you can do about it and that only vain people are interested in their looks, then the matter is a lot more complicated. Because you have been subjected to these messages from an early age on they have become firmly established in your subconscious mind. If you believe the first and second part, then you are also going to believe the third part.

No matter what anyone else tells you later on in life, you hang on to the first thing you were told. It is almost as if the first negative message got encapsulated in your mind and is now sealed off so that no further information can be added. As long as old messages go unchallenged they will rule your life. It is therefore necessary to open the capsule and take out that message and examine it carefully to determine to what extent it is valid.

Let's look first at the statement 'You don't look like much'. Please note that beauty is in the eye of the beholder. Beauty is relative. Just because your mother likes chubby children and you are skinny does not mean that you are ugly. It means that your mother prefers chubby children. If you went out and asked 100 men whether they preferred slim women or chubby ones, then 50 per cent would say they prefer slim ones and 50 per cent would say that they want someone with substance. So, it does not really matter whether you are slim or chubby, because there will always be someone who is interested in *you*. Provided you don't walk around with 'MISERYGUTS' written all over your face.

Note: You cannot please everyone, but you can kill yourself trying.

As to the second part – 'There isn't anything you can do about it,' – this is rubbish! Of *course* you can do something about presenting yourself in a favourable way. Have you ever seen models without their make-up on and their hair unstyled? They look quite unimpressive and very much like the girl next door. Nothing, or hardly anything, to write home about.

As a woman you have the big advantage of being able to make use of cosmetics if you want to. It need not be much. Look at your face. Which are the features that you can enhance by bringing them out more? Take the time to try out things. See what you look like with mascara, some eye-shadow. Apply foundation to your face and see what difference it makes when your skin looks even. Try lipstick. Get help from a friend whose judgement you respect and who knows how to apply make-up properly.

Check your hairstyle. Could you look better it you changed it? Try out something new. If you allowed yourself to find yourself attractive, what is the best thing you could do with your hair?

Check your clothing, but before you do, check your figure. Look for good points this time. Do you dress to bring out those good features? If not, then make a move now. Dowdy clothes are not going to lift your mood – they just demonstrate that you cannot be bothered to look after yourself. I am not talking expensive designer clothes here, I am saying that you can be well dressed even though you think you are too thin, fat, tall or short.

The third part – 'Only vain people are interested in their looks,' – is not true. You don't have to be a vain person to be interested in the way you present yourself. A vain person will spend hours in front of the mirror every day to check and re-check her appearance. Under no circumstances will she leave the house without make-up on. She relies heavily on her looks for her popularity and success in the general rush to find her Prince Charming. Because she cannot see that other factors such as charisma, capacity to give love, personality and serenity also play a part in finding him, she only concentrates on her outward appearance. In due course she will get her man. More than likely he is going to be someone who wants a presentable woman, but does not necessarily prize character or intelligence. This is fine, as long as you don't mind a man with low standards.

When beauty and looks are your only concern in life you will land yourself with an enormous problem once the looks have gone. You have put all your

eggs in one basket, and now the eggs have hatched and you are left with
an empty basket. If you have not cultivated other interests you are left
empty-handed once your heyday is over.

Being interested in your appearance does not have to dominate your life, but
it is important that you should know yourself. There is nothing wrong with
spending some time looking at yourself to determine where your strong and
weak points lie physically. There is nothing wrong with admitting that there are
features about yourself that you particularly like. That in itself does not make
you into a vain person. There is nothing wrong with emphasising your good
points. You may find your face too angular, but why not accentuate your eyes?
You may be overweight, but why hide your well-shaped calves? If you cannot
think of anything you like about your face or figure then it does not mean that
you are ugly, it just means you have not looked properly. Just look again.

As you begin to appreciate your *own* appearance, you will notice how your
envy of others disappears. Your new self-image makes you feel at one with those
well turned out, good-looking women in the street.

SCRIPT
**Everything I need to be attractive is already within me. I am helping my
beauty to emerge. I am taking an interest in my appearance. I am happy and
content. I open up to new positive attitudes towards myself and others. I
now perceive my own beauty and I delight in it. I feel beautiful, therefore
I am beautiful. I am happy when I look at other good-looking women
because they remind me that I am one of them.**

SHORT FORM
- **My eyes open to my own beauty. Great happiness spreads through my mind.**

It bothers me immensely that my husband is driving a smaller car than his colleagues

Why should this bother you when it does not bother your husband? Do you
think he owes it to his position to drive a bigger car? Or do you think he owes
it to *you* to demonstrate his position to others?

Some wives see their husbands as extensions of themselves. Their husband's success is their *own* success. The husband's advancement within the company is their *own* advancement. It is almost as if the wife's ego feeds off the husband's, as if there were an umbilical cord between the two so that the wife achieves her own aims through her husband's success.

This set-up should not be confused with that of giving moral support. Supporting another person means helping them get what *they* want, which is not necessarily the same thing that *you* want for them. If, however, you see the other person as an extension of yourself, you are manipulating them to achieve *your* aims without any regard to what they themselves want. This sort of manipulation can also be observed in parents who want to mould their children into becoming a certain type of person, to go into a certain type of profession. Tampering with others in this way is then pronounced to be an act of love when, really, it is only an act of self-gratification. You are not allowing the other person to be an individual. If, in addition, you make them feel guilty about wanting to go their own way, you distort their self-image and block their development.

Manipulation is the powerful tool of an impotent person. If you need to express yourself through someone else, you do not have the courage to live your own wishes. Maybe you were given to understand that your wishes did not count when you were a child, maybe you are not even aware that you have needs that have remained unfulfilled. It is this lack of self-knowledge that makes you powerless.

Manipulation is not necessarily a conscious process. The manipulating party can act in the genuine belief that they are furthering their partner's advancement. This does not alter the fact, however, that the underlying motives are selfish. Note, however, that I am not saying that having needs and wanting to fulfil them is selfish. It is perfectly OK, indeed, essential for your well-being to see to it that you get what you need. The selfish thing is to use someone else as vehicle for your own purposes.

If you want influence, you can achieve that through your *own* effort. If you want self-esteem, then get the real thing. Get the admiration of others by your *own* achievement. It is not fair to put this burden on to another person.

Don't hide behind statements like, 'I only want the best for you,' when what you really mean is that you only want the best for *yourself.* If this is so, why don't you go out and get it? Hassling and nagging is not going to get you anywhere, it is just going to estrange you from your husband. You are driving him away from you. He will no longer tell you what is happening at work, and, sooner or later, communication will break down.

When you are envious you feel that you have been short-changed by fate. You are furious because you do not get what you think is rightfully yours. The worst thing is that all the others seem to have it. It is as if everyone else got a big Christmas present and you only got a horrible little one. You measure your own value as a person by the value of the assets that surround you.

Wanting money and possessions as such is not wrong or immoral. It is perfectly acceptable to enjoy a good life and be financially comfortable. What is unacceptable is a situation where possessions are accumulated to make up for the emptiness inside. When possessions come to represent the externalisation of a yearning for fulfilment, when they become the purpose of life, then they are being misused. Envy is a clear sign that you assign this ersatz function to possessions.

Most of those people you envy have had to work for what they possess. It is incorrect to assume that it all fell into their laps. You get what you want and you pay the price. So if you want a better deal out of life then you personally have to provide more input. Look to the people who have achieved what they were after. Let other people's good fortune be an inspiration to you and understand that if they can achieve wealth so can you. Begin to use your talents. This is not a task you can delegate, this is your own, private responsibility – not your husband's.

You are a person with a will and a mind of your own and this is why *you* are responsible for what is happening in your life. Stop punishing your partner for your unhappiness. He is not in this world to provide you with a meaning for life. That is your job. You are a person in your own right and as such responsible for your own development, fulfilment and contentedness. Only *you* can give your life meaning – your personal, individual meaning. The best way to find a purpose in life is to start looking for it. As you begin to look, you have already found it. The question already contains the answer.

SCRIPT

I am striving for happiness and contentment. I take responsibility for my own personal well-being from now on. I am beginning to set myself targets that I meet through my own efforts. I am strong and confident. I am building up my self and my own life. Nothing can stop me now. I look at other people's achievements with interest and pleasure. They give me the confidence to proceed with my own plans. What others can achieve, I can achieve too. I set out on my new way with a happy heart. I listen to my inner voice, which guides me always. I know that there is always a way. The fact that I have been given a wish means that I have also been given a way of fulfilling that wish. I expect success and therefore I attract success.

SHORT FORM

- I look at other people's achievements with pleasure. My own good fortune is underway.
  or
  I am setting new goals now. Happiness creates ideas, ideas create wealth.

We have an open relationship, but I find I cannot cope with my girlfriend having affairs with other men

What was the original idea? It looks like both parties wanted to have their cake and eat it. To make an open relationship work, you must either love your partner very much or not all. The fact that you find it difficult to cope with your arrangement indicates that you are somewhere in between.

There are at least three ways in which this arrangement of an open relationship can come about.

- The idea can start as an idealistic enterprise in the beginning of the relationship where you see your capacity to love through a magnifying glass.
- Or you enter the relationship at a stage where your partner is still seeing another person and you agree to the arrangement, hoping it will resolve itself in time and you will be the one who is chosen as a permanent companion in the end.

- Or you just got together for convenience and sex, without the wish to commit yourself. No strings attached.

Equally, there are three reasons why this free arrangement backfires.

- Even somebody who has been completely swept off their feet will have to come down to earth after a while. After the initial period of love-sickness and honeymooning, reality overtakes you with breathtaking speed.

  The Spanish have a proverb: when a woman marries she exchanges the attention of many men for the inattention of one. Not altogether untrue, is it? And not only for women.

  Familiarity does not always breed contempt, but it certainly leads to insight and enlightenment and the original feelings are adjusted accordingly. The partner's faults are no longer forgiven that easily once the feet of clay have been revealed. The problem now is that, all of a sudden, you are not so sure any more whether you can really cope with your partner going off with someone else for the night. Your romantic view of her has come down a notch or two and your trust in her love for you has become a bit shaky at the same time. You would rather that she stayed with you and demonstrated that she likes you best. Things between you and her have changed, but the arrangement is still the same.
- You did not really want the open arrangement, but entered it in the hope that things would change after a while, but that change never came about. You cannot even complain about your misery because you were told clearly what the situation was from the very beginning and now you are stuck with your misery. Even though you are unhappy with the way things are, it may seem better than nothing, better than being alone, so you stay where you are, unhappy but unable to walk out.
- Even though you felt nicely detached when you started the relationship you do not feel like that any longer. Somehow, somewhere along the line you have become closer and more attached than you care to admit, and suddenly you are no longer 'cool'. You realise that you have become more possessive, that you would prefer your partner to commit herself more deeply to you.

You feel neglected and hurt and, though you may not feel like sleeping with someone else, you do it all the same, to get even. You have to prove that you do not care, that you are still the same cool dude you were in the beginning, but you know you are not. You are no longer having affairs because you *want* to, you are just using them as a weapon to hurt the other person.

In all these cases, reality does not fit your initial rules any more so there does not appear to be much sense in hanging on to the old arrangement. It is time to re-negotiate and adapt the old rules to the new circumstances. If your partner is unable or unwilling to change over to a steady relationship with you, you have two options. Either you walk out or you grin and bear it and stay with her.

If you choose the latter option you would do better to resign yourself to the state of affairs and suffer in silence, otherwise the relationship will become insufferable to both parties. Only you can decide whether this is the price you are prepared to pay for a relationship in which your partner is not prepared to commit herself. You may be better off cutting your losses and leaving – at least you will be able to look for someone who wants a steady relationship.

I am a second wife. I am jealous of my husband's first family because he gives them a lot of attention

You have probably heard everything about his first marriage, his first wife, the children and all the financial and emotional problems he went through until he finally broke away. You know everything about the time after the divorce, where he lived, the difficulties he had finding his own feet, up until the time he met you. Now you are married to him. To him and his first family, to be precise.

You know what things he did not like about his first wife, so you don't do them. You have spent hours listening to him talking about problems his ex-wife was creating during and after their divorce and you were hoping that you could now leave all this behind, but there simply does not seem an end to it. If there are any problems with the children, she calls him. If there are school fees to be paid or new school uniforms to be bought she calls him. She calls him for everything and anything, it seems, and you wonder whether it is ever going to stop. At the moment it certainly does not look like it and you are beginning to get impatient. You do not feel that you are getting the attention you are entitled to. After all, you are his wife now and you may even have children from this second marriage.

Every time she rings you get upset. A tug of war has developed where the wives each pull on one arm of the man in the middle. He is asked to divide his attention between his two families and this leaves him in a no-win situation. His first wife does not seem to understand that he has a new family now, his second wife is irritated because he cannot just shake off his past and start from scratch as if there had never been a first marriage.

Are you being reasonable about your demands for attention? Be honest with yourself. Does your husband really spend a lot of time dealing with his ex-wife or do you just feel very upset about the fact that he speaks with her at all?

There are two things you need to bear in mind. Firstly, your husband has spent some years – in some cases a considerable number of years – of his life with another person. This time has formed him to a certain extent and is part of him so there is no use pretending it never happened. There was a time when your husband loved his ex-wife and part of this love may well have survived the divorce. It is likely, too, that he still loves his children by his first wife. He has spent time with them and watched them grow up. He cared for them then and he still cares for them now. Would you want a husband who could light-heartedly sever these strings? If your husband is a loving person you cannot demand of him that he bestows this love exclusively on you.

Love is not like a cake where you get less because you have to share it with someone else. Love is an attitude, a source that continually flows. It is like water from a tap, the flow of which can be regulated and adjusted by turning the tap. Your husband may be opening the tap 100 per cent for you and 60 per cent for his first family, so just because they are getting the 60 per cent does not mean that you are getting only 40.

Secondly, your husband left his first family and later on chose to set up house with you. You must therefore be a woman who displays quite a few characteristics that are attractive to him. He chose to spend his future with you. Just because he still loves his first family does not mean he loves you any the less for it. Why don't you just try and trust him? The fact that he does not want to wipe out the past speaks *for* him rather than *against* him. He is obviously a man who stands by his commitments.

There is no point in fighting the situation, so why don't you accept it? Hate and jealousy won't do anything for your marriage, on the contrary.

If you really feel that your husband spends an inordinate amount of time dealing with his ex-family, speak to him about it. Do not accuse, just state facts. Say you would like to spend more time with him. Ask him whether there is anything the two of you can do to arrange more time together. Maybe you can agree on a family outing the following weekend to get the new concept going?

Have you ever met his ex-wife? Don't forget that you have only heard one side of the story. It may be very helpful if you two got on, so why not meet up for a coffee on neutral territory and get to know one another? You have nothing to lose and everything to gain. You may be surprised to find out that his ex-wife is just as worried about you as you are about her. You don't have to become best friends, but you will feel a lot better for knowing who this woman is at the other end of the line the next time she rings.

You chose to marry your husband for better or for worse. Give him support. He needs it.

SCRIPT

I chose my husband and my husband chose me. We have a good and loving relationship. I love him because he cares. He is doing his best to sort things out between himself and his first family. I send them my best wishes. I have confidence in myself. My inner strength enables me to help my husband through difficult times. We are working together. Our bond grows stronger and stronger every day. I trust him and he trusts me. I support him and he supports me. We are close and we care for one another. I am secure in the knowledge that I am being loved.

SHORT FORM

- The bond between me and my husband is strong. I support him and wish his first family all the best.

Part
Four

15 Hypnosis and Self-Hypnosis

▼ ▼ ▼ ▼

In Part One, I explained about the subconscious mind, how it works and how you can harness its powers to improve your life.

You will recall that it is the subconscious mind that acts as store-room for past experiences, recording both the event *and* the feelings that accompanied the incident at the time. These feelings can be either physical or emotional or both. For example, when your favourite aunt died you experienced the funeral (the physical event) *and* felt desperately sad (an emotional feeling); when you heard your parents screaming and shouting at each other (the physical event) you felt afraid (an emotional feeling) and had difficulties breathing (a physical feeling) because you felt so anxious. Your subconscious mind stores all these feelings and, the more frequently an event occurs, the more deeply the traces will be engraved in your memory.

We usually remember quite a few things from our childhood. We may still be able to describe what the playground looked like where we used to play at the age of four, we remember the first school we went to and some incidents that happened during that time. We may not be able to recall everything in great detail, but there will be little bits of information from the age of six upwards that are still present.

There are, however, also a great many things that we do not recall, things we would not know about if it was not for other people telling us about them. Your mother may vividly remember how you threw your soiled nappy at uncle Matthew when you were three, for instance, or your father may tell you how you plucked off the heads of all the tulips in the garden one day, but as we ourselves cannot remember these incidents *it is as if they have not happened.* It is only because we trust our parents not to have invented these stories that we believe they have taken place.

Consider for a moment, though, what happens if there has not been anyone else present at these times, no one to witness what you did, no one to see what happened to you. Because you don't remember, the incident is lost to your memory. Although the subconscious mind holds the memory of that event, the information can no longer be brought up into the conscious mind because it has been stored at a very deep level of the subconscious. Information and memories that are relevant to your present life need to be more easily accessible and are therefore kept where they can be returned to without much effort.

Information gets stored at a deep level for two reasons. Either the memories are no longer relevant for your adult life or they were so frightening and upsetting at the time that they needed to be repressed.

Repression is not a voluntary act, it happens automatically and functions as the mind's self-defence mechanism. When an incident is repressed you do not remember it any more and therefore it is like it never happened: that man you trusted never made advances, that dog you loved never got run over, that broom cupboard you got locked into never existed. Yet there are the feelings that went with the events at the time – guilt, shame, grief, terrible fear. Whatever they are, they will come out because feelings cannot be forgotten, even if the event itself is.

Feelings are always discharged, and they will be discharged until you have found the event that caused them in the first place. Only when you have made that link, only when you have connected up that feeling of guilt and shame to the incident of your favourite uncle touching you sexually can you stop feeling guilty and ashamed. Only when you have made that link between being locked up in the broom cupboard as punishment for something you did wrong when you were five and that feeling of panic you get as an adult every time you think you have made a mistake, only then will you be able to put that feeling of panic in its proper place, namely the past. Once this has been achieved you can then go on to start afresh and, with the help of ego-boosting suggestions, put your life on a new track.

Repression can manifest itself in various forms. Repressed memories can come out as anxiety states, panic attacks, depression or psychosomatic illnesses, to name but a few. Anyone who has ever had a panic attack will know how it seems to overcome you without any apparent reason. Depression makes you want to crawl in your bed and pull the blanket over your head and just cut yourself off from everything and everyone, but you don't know *why* you feel like that. If your well-being is that severely disrupted you will need outside help. Before you can begin a new life, you will have to sort out your past.

There is no point ignoring or denying the past. The faster you try to run away from it, the faster it will run after you. You cannot get rid of anything by running away. You have to turn around and face it; only then will it leave you alone for good. Find a good analytical hypnotherapist. He or she will help you find that subconscious cause of your problem in a relatively short period of time (usually between 8 and 15 sessions). To illustrate this point I will give an example of a client who overcame her problems by going through hypno-analysis.

This 45-year-old client, let's call her Marie, came to see me because she felt generally anxious, confused and out of control of her life. She had various phobias and a great fear of driving her car. She also reported that she always felt personally responsible for anything that went wrong in her family, even though it was not always her fault.

First of all, I introduced Marie to relaxation exercises, which she took to quite quickly. I made a self-hypnosis tape for her and asked her to use it at least once a day over the following three weeks. At the same time we wrote a Script to help her conquer her fear of driving (for the Script, see page 97).

After using the Script for two weeks, she reported that she had started using her car again. She pointed proudly to a Mini outside my practice and told me that she had chosen to come by car today, rather than walk. She was very pleased with her achievement, and rightly so.

To deal with her other problems I took her into analysis under hypnosis. She proved a very good subject. I asked her to recall events from her younger years and, in particular, her childhood and instructed her, once she was in hypnosis, to tell me about past events she found herself thinking about, no matter whether they seemed important or not.

Marie recalled a great number of incidents from her childhood years that had been fraught with problems. She was one of six children, with a mother who found it difficult to show affection and a father she admired greatly for his intelligence and popularity, but whom she feared at the same time for his violent temper when he got drunk, which happened frequently. She could not remember her parents ever praising her for anything.

During one session Marie recalled how her father came home drunk one evening. When he got in and found that his wife was not at home, he told the children to go up to their bedroom and stay there. Marie's mother had gone to the village to look for her husband, but Marie's father was furious at her absence. He suspected her of having an affair and started ranting and raving, getting his shotgun out and vowing that he was going to shoot her when she got back.

The children sat in their beds, terrified. Marie's little brothers and sisters started crying. Marie was very frightened herself, but felt she had to get out and warn her mother. She plucked up all her courage and went downstairs, but was stopped by her father who threatened her and ordered her to go back to bed immediately.

By this time Marie was so frightened that she obeyed. She went back upstairs, but could not go to sleep. She felt very upset and helpless, not knowing how to prevent the impending disaster.

Her mother finally got back to the house and looked through the window. Marie's father saw her and shouted at her to go away or he would shoot her. The mother went away and came back with a neighbour, upon which the father let them in and became more reasonable.

At the beginning of her next session, Marie reported that she had felt great relief at having recalled this scene and said she found it easier now to think about the past. I was pleased with this initial success, but suspected that there might be more to her problems than just that particular incident.

A few sessions later, Marie remembered a time when she was about ten years old when she had to sleep in the same bed with her father while they were away on a trip together. Marie got very agitated as she recalled how he had tried to touch her and, bursting into tears, she remembered how she had tried to fight him off, and how she had felt ashamed and guilty about the incident, but had been unable to tell anyone else about it. Marie continued crying for a little while, but then calmed down. She had felt guilty about this all her life, but now she started feeling angry at her father.

Once I had called her out of hypnosis, we had a final talk about what she had found out about herself. Marie told me that, all of a sudden, things were falling into place. She could see now why she had been feeling guilty all her life and that she now realised this was no longer necessary as she understood where this negative feeling originated. Her anxiety had disappeared.

If you have tried any of the exercises in this book, you already have a very good idea what it feels like to be hypnotised because the relaxation and imagination exercises are nothing but self-hypnosis. When someone else hypnotises you, you will probably just feel a bit more relaxed and a bit more detached than you do when you use self-suggestion. At no time will you be unconscious, though. A hypnotherapist cannot impose his or her will on you, nor make you do things you do not want to do nor make you reveal any secrets that you do not want to reveal. The hypnotherapist is dependent on your co-operation; only then can he or she help.

To find a good therapist, ring one of the big organisations who will advise you of a practitioner near you. Go for a consultation and have a good look at the therapist.

If you do not like the therapist, do not start with him or her. Trust your gut feeling. If it *feels* wrong it *is* wrong. You would be wasting your time and money and your chances of success would be considerably lessened if you started treatment with someone you did not trust.

Once you have started your sessions, see them through to the end. It is a well-known fact amongst therapists that clients experience a feeling of despondency and anxiety after a certain number of sessions. This is perfectly normal and just indicates that you are approaching the crucial issue. Psychoanalysis under hypnotherapy can be an invaluable tool for discovering the root of a problem.

Different people respond differently to hypnosis. Some people tell me after a session that they did not feel hypnotised at all, that they felt quite ordinary, as if they were just lying there listening to my voice. They may even feel disappointed because they were hoping that they would feel in a trance-like state, but this is not what hypnosis is about. The notion that you are in a trance is a myth that may have been created by films that show a fierce-looking man in a black cloak, dangling a watch in front of a good-looking young woman, who thereupon becomes bleary-eyed and proceeds to go off to stick a kitchen knife into her husband. Luckily there is no way anybody can be manipulated in this way through hypnosis.

Other people may experience a physical feeling of lightness or heaviness under hypnosis. Some people report that they felt quite normal during the session, but, once they opened their eyes again, felt as if they had been asleep for hours. Of course they have not, because they can remember quite clearly what I said to them during the session.

Whatever your personal experience is during hypnosis, whether you feel different from your normal waking state or not, has nothing to do with the outcome. I have had people assure me that they were not hypnotised at all, only to hear a week later that they stopped smoking.

Leave it to the therapist to decide whether you were 'under' or not. He or she will be able to tell by a number of signs whether you have reached the required state. If you are very tense, then you may require one or two sessions of relaxation to get you ready.

Hypnotherapy is worth your while in any case because it can help you activate your inner resources without having to resort to pills and tablets. Just one session of hypnosis with a therapist can help reinforce your own suggestions if you feel you need some help with the programme you find in this book.

Whatever you feed into your subconscious mind will determine how you experience your life, so why not make it something positive?

16 Guided Affective Imagery

▼ ▼ ▼ ▼

Another method of discovering and working through suppressed material is through a technique called Guided Affective Imagery (GAI). I use this method with clients who find it difficult to go into the hypnotic state or who have problems recalling their childhood.

Instead of being hypnotised, the client is just being relaxed. Rather than saying, 'You are relaxed now', the therapist will use the wording, 'Let your arms relax, allow your legs to become relaxed', and so on, the difference being that in the hypnotic induction, the client is told what is going to happen, whereas in GAI the client is encouraged to make it happen himself.

GAI works with symbolic representations of subconscious problems. The client is asked to imagine part of a landscape. This can be, for example, a meadow, a stream, a forest or a mountain. The therapist suggests one of these pictures, say the meadow, and asks the client to describe in great detail what sort of meadow he can see in his imagination. The client will come up with a spontaneous image that will allow insight into his attitudes and background. A meadow with soft green grass and lots of flowers, for example, reflects an emotionally stable personality, whereas a stretch of short, hard grass, fenced in by towering hedges, indicates the defence mechanism of an anxious and inhibited person.

Emotional problems are revealed in the symbolism of the landscape and any animals or objects in it. Other people can be perceived as far-away houses, indicating the detachment the client experiences from others. A dangerous situation may appear in GAI as a ferocious animal, like a lion or a monster. Symbolic representation in GAI often involves fantasy figures or fairy-tale-type characters. This depends very much on the individual client.

GAI not only allows the therapist insight into the client's emotional condition, it also gives her a tool to bring about positive change and to combat long-standing fears by helping the client confront them in his images. To illustrate the way GAI works here are a few examples.

CASE 1

One of my clients, who suffered from depression and anxiety, visualised a meadow that was surrounded by a high, thorny hedge that prevented her from seeing anything beyond her little patch of grass.

She felt oppressed by this confined space, but at the same time anxious about what might be outside. I encouraged her to go along the hedge and look out for a gap, which she eventually discovered. After a lot of hesitation she consented to crawl through the gap and venture beyond her confines to see whether her fears about the outside world were justified. She was surprised to find quite a pleasant open landscape and, although she kept close to her own territory (her bordered meadow), she also felt a sense of achievement in having taken this step into the unknown. In her next session she reported that she had ventured into town to do some window-shopping, something she had not done in a long time.

CASE 2

Another client had the problem of not being able to see things through in his life. As soon as a problem appeared, he abandoned his project and, as a consequence, felt disappointed and angry at himself. He had a negative self-image that prevented him from persisting and his lack of stamina in turn reinforced his negative self-image. He was virtually trapped.

In his imagination he saw a great big mountain at the end of his meadow and mentioned that it might be very pleasant to see the view from the top, but as soon as he had reached the foothills and realised how steep the ascent was, he was ready to give up.

I encouraged him to look around for some tools that could help him tackle the ascent and he eventually found climbing gear. He slowly began to go up the mountain, describing how he progressed as he went along.

At one point he began to feel tired and sat down to have a rest. Then he decided he could not go on. I asked him if there was anything or anyone who could help him climb the remaining distance to the top. He replied quite spontaneously that he could actually see another man who had already reached the top. He shouted up to ask for his assistance. The other man let down a strong rope that the client tied around his body and, with the man pulling from above and himself climbing vigorously, he finally reached the top, from where he enjoyed a magnificent view. At the same time he experienced a great feeling of happiness and fulfilment. When he opened his eyes again he told me that he felt exhausted, as if he had climbed that mountain in reality.

After several more sessions of successfully tackling other obstacles and finding out in the process what lay at the bottom of his lack of persistence, he found himself able to translate his imagined successes into reality. He decided to finally tackle an exam he had been postponing for quite a while, and the last I heard from him was that he passed it and has now gone into a new job that gives him great pleasure and satisfaction.

Case 3

A young girl of 21 came into my practice one day. She suffered from anxiety and had been on tranquillisers since she was 16.

As she was very nervous, I spent the first session taking her through relaxation exercises, which I asked her to practise at home. In the second session, we started with GAI, which seemed to come quite naturally to her. She could 'see' the scenes in vivid colours and in great detail.

A path from her meadow led her to a house in the middle of nowhere. There was no one else around so I asked her to enter the house and tell me what she found inside. She first went into a kitchen that was all white, very tidy without anything lying around. When she opened the cupboards, however, she found them full of food. The living room was very comfortable, with cosy armchairs and sofas, but without any pictures on the walls.

She then went up a narrow staircase and came to two small bedrooms, one of which was totally empty. The other bedroom had an empty pram in it, but no baby. Next to the pram there was a chair. Otherwise the room was empty. No toys, no baby clothes.

She also observed that, although it was very bright outside and although the house had big windows, it was very dark inside.

I asked her to look for a cellar. She went outside and found a shabby door next to the entrance door, which she refused to open. She felt that this was the house of a man who only used it on weekends. She did not think it would be right to go down into the cellar because, as she told me, it was the 'most private place of the house'.

In one of the following sessions I persuaded her to actually go down into the basement. As she was very worried about doing this, I suggested she was taking a magic sword with her that she could use to defend herself should it become necessary.

As she descended the stairs, she heard an animal growling and then saw a huge dog-like creature approaching her, baring its fangs. She was terrified, but began to use her sword to fend off her attacker, bringing her weapon down on the dog until it lay dead on the ground. She started sobbing and declared that the animal had been her father, who had terrorised her family all his life. He had been an alcoholic who would come home at night, smashing up the place and beating up any family member he could get hold of.

The explanation for the empty pram turned out to be the symbolic image of an abortion the client had had a couple of years ago, which she felt very guilty about.

Once she had started seeing these connections, she realised that this house was a symbol of her own life, with the basement being her childhood. She suddenly understood why she had assumed that the house was a man's. Throughout her life she had experienced women as weak and helpless and men as the group of people who were in control and owned things. It was therefore not possible that she, as a woman, owned anything, not even her own body. She had given in to pressure from her boyfriend to have the abortion although she had wanted the baby.

Her anxiety attacks ceased once she had fought the battle with her father and she is now gradually coming off her tranquillisers under her doctor's supervision.

Summary

GAI, just like hypnosis and self-hypnosis, makes use of the powers of the subconscious mind. Some people are worried about the fact that they are only 'making things up', but when you consider how many different types of houses you could imagine and how you pick one particular version, then it becomes evident that your choice is dictated by your emotional state and by your past. The image you select is always related to something that really happened in your life, albeit in the disguised form of a symbol. The imaginary set-up of GAI allows the subconscious mind to express itself in a way that may appear less threatening to the client than remembering the actual incident.

As you will remember, the subconscious mind does not distinguish between imagination and reality. Once you have dealt with an upsetting event in the past it loses its negative power over you. Whether you do this symbolically or by re-living the actual event during hypnosis does not influence the beneficial outcome.

Positive Thinking is just another tool to change your life for the better and it works along the same lines. Use the powers of your subconscious mind to your advantage, and you can achieve whatever you desire.

> *Note: It does not matter how the wind blows. The only thing that matters is how you set your sail.*

Notes

▼　▼　▼　▼

- The harder you try to avoid something, the less you can do it.
- The best time to act on new resolutions is now (not the 1st January).
- When your will-power conflicts with your imagination, your imagination will always win out.
- Never give up.
- Once the facts-memory-behaviour chain has been established, it works automatically.
- Feelings that have been stored away in the memory will always be discharged as behaviour.
- The more often a message is repeated, the deeper it is impressed on the subconscious.
- The stronger the emotion accompanying an event, the stronger that emotion is impressed on the subconscious.
- The quality of your thoughts determines the quality of your life.
- Whatever you send out to others will come back to you like a boomerang.
- A person who is interested is interesting.
- It is of fundamental importance that you look after yourself and work on achieving happiness for yourself.
- Every achievement has started as an idea.
- Physical tension creates mental tension. Mental tension creates physical tension.
- The harder you try to relax the less you can do it.
- You can because you think you can.
- Other people cannot read your mind.
- You are your own best friend. Be kind to yourself.
- The outside reflects the inside.

- The more will-power you employ to reach your target the less you can do it.
- Just because you cannot see a way does not mean there is no way.
- Don't believe in miracles. Rely on them.
- Things are meant to go right.
- What you can do once you can do again.
- You have to play the pools to win.
- Whatever you spend a lot of time thinking about will become bigger.
- Everyone has rights as well as duties.
- Believe in yourself.
- It is OK to say what you want.
- You cannot please everyone, but you can kill yourself trying.
- It does not matter how the wind blows. The only thing that matters is how you set your sail.

Further Reading

Louise L. Hay, *Heal Your Body*, Eden Grove Editions, 1989.

——, *You Can Heal Your Life*, Eden Grove Editions, 1988.

Norman Vincent Peale, *The Power of Positive Thinking*, Cedar, 1953.

Vera Peiffer, *Positively Fearless*, Thorsons, 2001.

——, *Principles of Hypnotherapy*, Thorsons, 1996.

——, *Principles of Stress Management*, Thorsons, 1996.

James Redfield, *The Celestine Prophecy*, Warner Books, 1994.

Index